GOVERNORS OF THE OLD NORTHWEST

THE

TERRITORIAL GOVERNORS

OF THE

OLD NORTHWEST

A STUDY IN TERRITORIAL ADMINISTRATION

BY
DWIGHT G. McCARTY

PUBLISHED AT IOWA CITY IOWA IN 1910 BY
THE STATE HISTORICAL SOCIETY OF IOWA

THE
TORCH
PRESS
CEDAR RAPIDS
IOWA

EDITOR'S INTRODUCTION

As a geographical area the Iowa country became a part of the United States through the purchase of the Province of Louisiana in 1803: and so territorial descent is traced through the District of Louisiana, the Territory of Louisiana, and the Territory of Missouri.

On the other hand the political inheritances of Iowa, which are Anglo-American, were transmitted through the Territories of the Old Northwest — especially the Northwest Territory, the Indiana Territory, the Territory of Michigan, and the original Territory of Wisconsin. Thus the study of the evolution of the government and administration of these Territories forms a logical introduction to the constitutional and political history of Iowa. And it is from this viewpoint that The State Historical Society of Iowa has undertaken to publish a book on the Territorial Governors of the Old Northwest.

As worked out by Mr. McCarty under the direction of The State Historical Society of

Iowa, this volume is neither a source book nor a book of biography, but a brief outline of the development of Territorial government and administration in the Old Northwest.

Since a volume on Henry Dodge is being prepared for the Iowa Biographical Series, Chapter X of this book on *Governors Dodge and Doty and the Territory of Wisconsin* has been curtailed by the author. The government and administration of the Territory of Wisconsin will receive adequate treatment in the book on Henry Dodge.

Benj. F. Shambaugh

Office of the Superintendent and Editor
The State Historical Society of Iowa
Iowa City 1910

AUTHOR'S PREFACE

The Old Northwest occupies a peculiar position in American history. Rich in the traditions of the past, when nations struggled for supremacy along its borders, it was left at the feet of the original thirteen States by the receding waves of the Revolution — a vast wilderness of boundless resources, waiting for the magic touch of civilization. The original thirteen States were then just beginning to round out into a unified National life. This life was tentative and uncertain at first; but after the critical period was passed it burst out of its old confines and spread over the western country with a joyous abandon that threatened to outstrip the forms and traditions of the old régime.

It was an eminently practical evolution that within a few decades transformed the wilderness of the Old Northwest into the populous and flourishing States of Ohio, Indiana, Illinois, Michigan, and Wisconsin. The genesis and early development of the Northwest Territory are, therefore, strategic points from which a correct study of western American institutions and their growth must of necessity

begin.   Nearly all of the States of the West have
had to pass through a preparation for statehood —
a tutelage more or less rigorous, depending upon
local conditions and the rapidity of advancement.
Many characteristic features of our present systems
of State government are the product of Territorial
conditions.

The undeveloped country stretching westward
from the Alleghanies was like an ambitious and
headstrong child, and needed the guidance of a
paternal hand during its adolescence. It is this
fact that has given a distinctive character to the
form of Territorial government. A strong Governor, with plenary powers and no responsibility
except to the National government from which he
receives his appointment, has been the center and
mainstay of Territorial government in the United
States. A study of the governments of the various
Territories in the Old Northwest from the standpoint of the Governors will therefore shed light upon
the influences which moulded the character and
destiny of Territories and Commonwealths.

It is the purpose of the pages that follow to
present an outline history of Territorial government
in the Old Northwest, from the time of American
acquisition down to the admission of Wisconsin into

the Union as a State in 1848, as revealed especially in the activities of the Territorial Governors. The first two chapters deal with early conditions in the Old Northwest, and with the first attempts at government. The third and fourth chapters consist respectively of an analysis of the main provisions of the Ordinance of 1787, and of a statement of the powers, functions, and importance of the Territorial Governor. The remaining chapters constitute a comparative study of the forms and processes of administration as actually worked out in the original Northwest Territory and in the Territories of Indiana, Illinois, Michigan, and Wisconsin.

Throughout, the object has been to characterize rather than to present a detailed history — to indicate the real forces at work in the beginnings of Territorial government and to point out the important part played by the Governor.

The material for these pages has been gathered largely from original sources. Notes and references to both original and secondary sources have been liberally employed, not only to indicate the authority for statements of fact but also to guide the reader who may desire to make further investigations into subjects which necessarily receive little more than mention in the present volume.

It has been some nine years since this monograph was begun — most of the work having been done either while the author was a student at Harvard University or during vacations when there was opportunity to visit the various archives where the rich collections of sources for western history are to be found. In a somewhat abridged form the study was originally presented as a master's thesis at Iowa College, Grinnell, Iowa, in 1904. Since that time the manuscript has been enlarged and revised; but the exactions of a busy law practice and the burden of other duties have delayed its completion.

In this connection I desire to express my indebtedness to The State Historical Society of Iowa which has made possible the publication of the book at this time; and especially am I under obligation to Professor Benj. F. Shambaugh, Superintendent and Editor, for his friendly personal interest, his critical editing of the manuscript, and his aid in seeing the volume through the press. Mr. Dan E. Clark, Research Assistant in The State Historical Society of Iowa, has rendered very valuable assistance in verifying quotations and references and in securing uniformity in the notes. My grateful acknowledgments for helpful suggestions and encouragement are also due to Professor Allen Johnson, Professor

Jesse Macy, Professor Albert Bushnell Hart, Professor Edward Channing, Professor Frederick J. Turner, and to others who have generously aided me from time to time.

Dwight G. McCarty

Emmetsburg, Iowa

CONTENTS

enemies and made the frontier, always exposed at best, doubly difficult to defend.

The colonists, who by persistent industry had built up permanent settlements and prosperous estates on the coast, were slow to take possession of this rich western country. In fact the English did not succeed in gaining a permanent foothold on the shores of the Atlantic until more than a hundred years after the discoveries of Columbus; and the Revolution found their settlements still practically confined to the seaward side of the Alleghanies. On the other hand, before the founding of Jamestown or the landing of the Pilgrims, the Spaniards had penetrated far into the heart of the continent and had made scattered settlements in Central America and Florida; while the French had possessed themselves of Canada before the end of the seventeenth century and were exploring, trapping, and settling in the upper Mississippi Valley.

The English were slow to move westward; but their settlements were of a permanent nature. The French, on the other hand, explored much, traded with the Indians, and settled little.

From the first France tenaciously maintained her claim to the western territory. She built a chain of forts connecting the St. Lawrence and the Mississippi, made alliances with the neighboring Indian tribes, and sought in every way to protect her extended frontier possessions. England, becoming alive to the situation, enlisted the support of her

I

THE OLD NORTHWEST

To the thirteen colonies clustered on the Atlantic seaboard the "western country" was a wild, unexplored region — a vague margin on a well-known map. But this country, later known as the Old Northwest, had a physiographic unity of its own. Comprising the region northwest of the River Ohio, it was bounded on the East by the Alleghany Mountains, on the West by the Mississippi River, and on the North it found its natural limitations in the great lake region. Thus it embraced a beautiful portion of the Mississippi Valley, with moderate temperature, abundant rainfall, fertile soil well adapted for agriculture, and rich mineral resources. It was a level plain covered with luxurious forests and broad prairies of waving grass, abounding in game.

The Great Lakes at the north, the large rivers that formed its boundaries, and the numerous tributary streams that flowed through this country were admirable water highways which were of the greatest assistance to the pioneer in his long journey through the wilderness. They also served as a much needed means of communication and formed an avenue for the transportation of supplies. But they likewise furnished a ready approach for wily growing colonies in the endeavor to humble her haughty rival. The wars waged on European soil between the mother countries found their counterparts in fierce border warfare in the New World. The English gained little ground until the capture of Fort Duquesne in 1758 gave them the key to the Mississippi region, and the victory of Wolfe on the Plains of Abraham in 1759 made an entering wedge into Canada.[1]

This continuous strife was finally terminated by the Treaty of Paris in 1763, by which France ceded to Great Britain all Canada and all of her territory east of the Mississippi River — with the exception of New Orleans and a small strip of adjacent land. Spain, the luckless ally of France in this struggle, was forced to give up Florida to the conqueror. By a secret treaty in November of the preceding year France had transferred to Spain New Orleans and all of her possessions west of the Mississippi known as Louisiana.[2]

France having been eliminated from North America, Great Britain became the dominating power, with Spain in control across the Mississippi. England had taken her place as a great world power and was now undergoing governmental transformations which began to be manifested in her colonial policy. The colonies were to be ruled with a rod of iron, and coercive measures which foreshadowed the Revolution were inaugurated.

The King's Proclamation of 1763 established

boundaries and governments in the newly acquired
territory, and forbade the granting of any land "beyond the heads or sources of any of the rivers which
fall into the Atlantic Ocean from the west or northwest".[3]   Any such exclusive policy that consigned
the region west of the Alleghanies to the Indians was
doomed to failure, for the colonists were already beginning to turn toward the West.   Several of the
colonies, moreover, claimed parts of this region by
virtue of old grants from the Crown.   Continual
repression of the colonies only nursed rebellion; and
the inevitable result was the Revolutionary War.
The valiant fight of the colonists for independence
is a matter of history, and the part that the sturdy
backwoodsmen played has often been told.   Under
the leadership of George Rogers Clark the fearless
band of "Kentucky Long Knives" conquered the
wilderness territory and saved the West for the
Americans.[4]

The fact that the Americans had conquered and
successfully held possession of this vast territory
enabled the commissioners to name the Mississippi
as the western boundary of the United States when
the treaty of peace was at last signed in 1783. It was
the permanent acquisition of the territory northwest
of the River Ohio that prepared the way for the
great westward movement.

Nor was this constant warring of nationalities
without an important influence upon the history of
the Northwest.   France was there first and stamped

her policy and personality so firmly on the region
that they were continually cropping out to harass
the later American advance. It has been suggested
that it was the encumbrances inherited from the
French régime that retarded the development of
Michigan and Wisconsin and postponed for so long
their final assimilation as a part of the Union; while
Ohio, which was furthest removed from these early
influences and more directly in touch with the English Colonies, was from the first essentially American.[5]

Moreover, the Spaniards were constantly in-
triguing against the Americans, striving to undermine their allegiance and gain their trade and territory. Their tactics are well illustrated by the
attempts to induce Kentucky to separate from the
Union, and the interference with western trade by
controlling the mouth of the Mississippi River and
impeding its free navigation.[6]

The English also maintained a policy that was
at all times inimical to the progress of the American
settlement. They saw a rich country and a profit-
able fur trade slipping away from them, and they
strove to strengthen their hold on the land by making
allies of the Indian tribes.[7] Even where their plans
failed, the mistakes and abuses of their often incompetent officers in dealing with the Indians produced
a stumbling block that was continually cumbering
the path of the later pioneers. The Old Northwest
was the outpost battlefield of the Revolution; and

though the struggle was as decisive there as in the colonies, yet the influence of the former régime lingered much longer. The British held on to their frontier posts long after the date set for their relinquishment; and even after they had retired they continued to exercise a sinister influence from across the border until long after the War of 1812.[8]

But more formidable than European intruders and their foreign tendencies was the dreaded Indian. Accustomed to Nature's abundance and contented only when roaming unhampered through vast areas where he might hunt and trap and camp as he chose, the Indian resisted the steady advance of the White Man. With savage cunning he would pounce upon the isolated and unsuspecting settler, murder him and his family, and burn his cabin to the ground. Roving bands stole horses and cattle from the settlers and committed the most atrocious depredations at the settlements on the frontier. When on the war path they left a trail of blood and utter desolation, and spread terror throughout the region. The Indians were indeed the most persistent and dreaded foes of the pioneers, and they were aided and encouraged in their hostility by the English and Spanish along the borders.

Constant trouble and warfare were the inevitable result of these conditions in the Northwest Territory, and disturbances of one form or another prevailed throughout the whole period of western settlement.

In the manner of its development the Old Northwest was a unit. Though there were naturally local
variations, yet in its general trend the movement
toward settlement in the Northwest as a whole dif-
fered widely from that of the country south of the
Ohio. As Mr. Roosevelt has so well shown, the
Southwest was settled by the individual initiative of
the backwoodsmen, who with their axes and long
guns forced their way through the vast wilderness,
conquered it in their own way, and constructed their
own form of government independent of the parent
State; while, on the other hand, the Northwest was
developed by the Nation as a whole — the government
troops leading the way, the settler following; while
the form of government was prescribed by the United
States from the beginning.[9]

Moreover the presence of these two tendencies
on different sides of the Ohio had in itself an important influence on the Northwest. The Southwest
was developed first, and it was the same hardy backwoodsmen from Virginia and Kentucky who conquered the Northwest and thus made possible its settlement along natural lines. The first settlers were
also from the South, and the greater part of them
were widely scattered over the whole region — few of
them living in the small French towns.[10]

The first comers were mostly adventurers and
squatters who persisted in putting their cabins on
the Indian lands in spite of the vigilance of the
troops. But as soon as the country was opened up

for settlement this condition of affairs was modified by an infusion of new immigration from New England and the Middle States.[11]

Beginning with the founding of Marietta in 1788 by the ''New Pilgrims'' from New England and continuing with the influx of settlers from Pennsylvania and adjacent States, the influence of the National government commenced to dominate the Northwest. The spirit of western democracy was larger than sectional influences, and it slowly but surely merged the earlier individualistic tendencies of the frontiersman into an unconscious compromise. And, as it will appear later, it was this same colonization compromise which, under the guidance of the Territorial Governor, gave rise to some of the most characteristic institutions and conditions connected with western development.

The great magnet that attracted settlers to the Territory was land, which was cheap and plenty. Moreover, traders and squatters, adventurers and settlers alike were willing to undergo frontier privations in order to secure a piece of land which they might call their own. They traveled long distances and through vast stretches of wilderness, and when they settled down it was usually with their nearest neighbor a long way off.

These characteristic facts and conditions of the frontier had important results. They gave the frontiersman a broader outlook and a more democratic spirit, increased his self-confidence and individual initiative, and developed rugged persistence of character. Economically he became more independent and politically more democratic. The old provincialism was shaken off on the broad prairies, and the free, buoyant, western democracy took its place.

Such, in brief, are some of the elements that were present in the growth and development of the Old Northwest. The pioneer not only had to hew his way through the forest and break the prairie sod, but he was compelled to clear away the blackened stumps of foreign occupation and pull out the weeds of foreign influence. And all the while he must stand guard to protect his home from the incursions of an ever relentless Indian foe. These were real obstacles to progress, and yet they were the means of developing character. Strongly impressed upon the Territory at the very beginning, these conditions persisted throughout its history as a vital influence upon its life and spirit.

Self-reliance, strength, energy, and a broader vision are the characteristic traits that were born of the taming of the wilderness. Undaunted by hardship or danger, the sturdy figure of the pioneer stands in the forefront, typifying the nature of the development of the West.

EARLY ATTEMPTS AT GOVERNMENT

The early government of the Old Northwest as the foundation for the later governmental system of the Territories is worthy of careful consideration. Such government as there was any necessity for under the French and English régimes was mainly paternal and military. It is therefore interesting to trace the evolution of the system built up by the Americans.

Within a very short time after General George Rogers Clark had won the country northwest of the Ohio, the State of Virginia, on the basis of its claim to that region, passed an act establishing the "County of Ilinois", for the purpose of providing a temporary form of government and affording necessary protection to the inhabitants. The act was to remain in force for only twelve months. It empowered the Governor of Virginia, with the consent of the Council, to appoint a County Lieutenant, who in turn was to appoint and commission such deputy commanders and militia officers as he should think necessary. The County Lieutenant had a general pardoning power, except in cases of murder and treason, when appeal was taken to the Governor and legislature respectively of Virginia. He was required to call the citizens of the various districts together for the purpose of electing persons to fill those civil offices to which the people had been accustomed. These officials were to exercise jurisdiction and conduct themselves in conformity with the laws then existing among them, and were to "be paid for their services in the same manner as such expenses" had previously been "borne, levied, and paid in that county".[12]

It is obvious that in this way the legislature hoped to avoid many of the difficulties of inaugurating a new system, and to make the transition as smooth as possible. "By preserving local customs and local organs of government, and by introducing few new officials, it was hoped that the change could be accomplished with little disturbance."[13] In order to more effectually protect the country, the Governor of the State was empowered by the act to raise and equip five hundred men to garrison the posts in Illinois.

On the 12th day of December, 1778, Patrick Henry, then Governor of Virginia, appointed Colonel John Todd as the County Lieutenant. He wrote an elaborate and statesmanlike letter of instructions on the inside of the front cover of a record-book, which was then sent on its long journey through the wilderness and delivered to John Todd as his credentials.[14] It was in this book that Todd later made the entries which give us our chief knowledge of the administration of the county government.

John Todd was born in Pennsylvania in 1750. He was educated in a classical academy, spent some time in the study of law, and had considerable military and legislative experience.[15] He was not unfamiliar with frontier conditions, and seems to have possessed the energy required to administer the affairs of the office to which he had been appointed.

It was in the spring of the year 1779 that Todd arrived at Kaskaskia and with characteristic vigor began his work. Governor Henry had written a letter to George Rogers Clark, who continued in command of the troops in Illinois, apprising him of the appointment of Todd as the one in authority in civil affairs and requesting his coöperation in promoting the best interests of the county.[16] Clark was glad to be relieved of the civil duties which, in the unorganized condition of the country, had become somewhat burdensome.[17] The people were called together and judges,[18] a sheriff, clerks, and other officers were elected. A majority of these officers, judging from their names, appear to have been Frenchmen. Military commissions were also issued, and among the recipients were many who had already been elected judges.[19] The lack of good material for officers is not unusual in such a frontier community, and so duplication is not surprising where a few men are apt to be the natural leaders.

The new government seemed to work smoothly enough for a time. The presence of Clark and his troops kept the Indians quiet, and there was little disturbance to make active interference among the settlers necessary. The courts, composed of easy-going Frenchmen as judges, had little to do — a condition which they construed as meaning that there was no necessity for meeting. Todd, however, issued an order requiring them to hold the regular sessions; and the *Record-Book* discloses regular meetings for some time thereafter, although at all but four of them no business except adjournment was transacted.[20]

There were, nevertheless, certain conditions which made the government unstable. The scattered population made administration difficult, and the dissatisfaction with the innovation of self-government on the part of the indifferent French population undermined the efficiency of the system. Hard times, the failure of crops, the depreciation of the almost worthless American currency, and the troubles growing out of the disposition of the public lands, all added to the difficulties of the situation. Todd tried his best to overcome them and did succeed in some measure in mitigating the hardships, especially with regard to the land troubles.[21] He found it very difficult to get supplies for the troops; and he was finally compelled to resort to forced levies,[22] which gave rise to misunderstandings between the civil and military authorities and bred discontent among the inhabitants until in the end there was open antagonism.[23] Under such conditions it was impossible to maintain authority; and so, late in the fall of 1779 or in the spring of 1780, Colonel Todd left the country.

It would be unjust to attribute to John Todd the blame for the unfortunate situation. It was rather the inevitable result of the confused and inharmonious conditions existing in the county itself. In fact one of the militia officers who was the most pronounced in his denunciation of Todd, some time later in an apologetic letter, admitted that he had entirely failed to appreciate the true condition of affairs.[24] While it is true that the hardships of the people were very great, yet it is probable that much of the criticism of Colonel Todd was altogether unwarrantable.

Colonel George Rogers Clark left the Illinois country about the same time, and there is some uncertainty as to whether Richard Winston or Thimothé Demunbrunt was the deputy and lieutenant-commandant left in charge of affairs.[25] The very uncertainty on this point is an indication of the confusion existing in the county. The feeling between the military and civil officers became still more intense and they hampered each other at every step.[26] Thus government in the county soon became so demoralized and impotent that it was openly defied by the inhabitants. The Virginia authorities, distracted by important events at home, had given it little support, and they now began the gradual withdrawal of the troops.[27]

The government of the Illinois County as provided for in the act of the Virginia legislature expired in 1781.[28]   The commission appointed in 1783 reported that the French inhabitants were not friendly to Virginia, that the Indians were going over to the British, and that the Illinois County was in such a desperate condition that stringent measures must immediately be taken if Virginia expected to retain control.[29]   But Virginia did nothing, either because of the difficulties at home, or the expense, or because she had already conditionally ceded her claim on this region to the United States government.

The lawlessness in the frontier country at this time is well described in the petition of Carbonneaux, the Prothonotary and Notary Public for the Illinois settlements. He complained that "they are wholly without law or government; that their magistrates, from indolence or sinister views, having for some time been relax in the execution of their office, are now altogether without authority; that crime of the greatest enormity may be committed with impunity, and a man be murdered in his own house & no person regard it; that they have no sheriff nor prison; and, to crown the general confusion, that many people have made large purchases of three or four hundred leagues, and are endeavoring to have themselves established lords of the soil as some have done in Canada, and have settlements made on these purchases composed of a set of men wholly subservient to their views." [30]

Thus left to its fate and torn by internal disturbances it is not strange that anarchy prevailed in the Illinois County. The temporary government had been moderately efficient while it lasted, although it disclosed the difficulty of applying complete self-government to such conditions. The test had also shown the possibilities of the American form of government, and it now only needed persistent assertion to make the American idea dominate the West. It was, to be sure, a little early for the experiment, but the forces were gathering in a new quarter, and in a very short time the strong hand of the National government was to be felt in the country northwest of the Ohio.

III

THE ORDINANCE OF 1787

The necessity for some sort of government for the unorganized western country had become very urgent. A number of States, including Virginia, had ceded their western lands to the United States and the others were on the verge of doing so. Petitions in great numbers, praying for relief and assistance, were coming in to Congress from both French and Americans in the distracted West.[31] The Congress of the Confederation had in fact made attempts to provide a form of government, but the resulting measures were not given a trial.[32]

A New England immigration society, called the "Ohio Company", organized in 1786 and composed mostly of Revolutionary soldiers who were anxious to settle on the lands west of the Alleghanies, presented a petition to Congress and sent representatives to plead their cause.[33] This petition seems to have hastened the action of Congress, and to a certain extent it may have affected the nature of the enactment which was designated to guarantee a free and stable government to prospective settlers in the West.

And so, on July 13, 1787, while the Federal Constitutional Convention was still in session at

Philadelphia, the Congress of the Confederation passed the famous Ordinance of 1787, which was entitled "An Ordinance for the Government of the Territory of the United States, north-west of the river Ohio."[34]   There has been considerable controversy as to the authorship of this Ordinance and as to the motives which prompted its enactment,[35] but there is no doubt of the wisdom of its provisions or of the permanence of the policy it inaugurated.

In general tone the instrument was one that would inspire confidence.   It contained six "articles of compact between the original states, and the people and states in the said territory", in the nature of a Bill of Rights, guaranteeing civil and religious liberty and the enjoyment of the fundamental principles of government which were forever to "remain unalterable, unless by common consent".   It also prohibited slavery in the Territory, encouraged public education, and provided for the establishment and admission into the Union of new States on an equal footing with the older Commonwealths.   Moreover, the Ordinance contained a clear and workable system of law on the descent and transfer of property, thus firmly establishing once for all one of the basic elements in the life of the new country.

The initial stage of government and the means of administration provided by the Ordinance were comparatively simple.   There was to be a Governor appointed by Congress for a term of three years, who must reside in the district which he was to gov-

ern and have a freehold estate of one thousand acres
of land therein while in office. A Secretary was to
be chosen by Congress for a term of four years with
the same requirement as to residence, and he was
to have a freehold estate of five hundred acres. Finally, Congress was to appoint three Judges to hold
office during good behavior, each of whom was to
reside in the district and have a freehold estate of
five hundred acres. It was provided that any two
of the Judges should constitute a court having common law jurisdiction.

The Governor and Judges were given power to
adopt such laws of the original States as they
thought necessary, and these laws were to remain
in force in the district unless disapproved of by
Congress. The Governor was authorized to appoint
magistrates and other civil officers in each county or
township. He was empowered to make proper provisions for the enforcement of the laws, and to lay
out parts of the district into counties and townships
from time to time as circumstances required. He
was also to be Commander-in-Chief of the militia,
and to appoint and commission all military officers
below the rank of general officers, the latter being
commissioned by Congress. Such was the machinery
provided for the administration of the first stage of
Territorial government.

The Ordinance further made provision for an
enlargement of this "temporary" government to
meet the demands of growth and settlement. When

there were five thousand free male inhabitants of full
age in the district, the Governor was to call an election for Representatives in a General Assembly.
Each Representative must have been "a citizen of
one of the United States three years" and a resident
of the district, or he must have been a resident of the
district for three years. Furthermore, he must own
in fee simple two hundred acres of land within the
district. Representatives were to hold office for two
years. The qualifications for electors of Representatives were a freehold estate of fifty acres, previous
citizenship in one of the States, and residence in the
district, or a like property qualification and residence
for two years in the district.

At a time and place designated by the Governor
the newly elected Representatives were to meet and
nominate ten persons, all residents of the district,
five of whom Congress was to appoint and commission as members of a Legislative Council to hold
office for five years. The property qualification for
members of the Council was a freehold estate of five
hundred acres.

The Territorial legislature in the second stage
of government, therefore, was to consist of the Governor, the Legislative Council, and the House of
Representatives; and it was invested with the authority to make all laws necessary for the good government of the Territory. The legislature was also
entrusted with the power of defining and regulating
the powers and duties of the magistrates and other

civil officers, and with the right to elect a Delegate who should represent the Territory in Congress. It was provided, however, that all bills, having passed by a majority in both the House of Representatives and the Council, should be referred to the Governor, and that without his assent no bill should become a law. The power to convene, prorogue, and dissolve the legislature was vested in the Governor.

Such is a brief summary of the main provisions of the Ordinance of 1787 — with special emphasis on those provisions which throw light on the powers and duties of the Governor. It is obvious that the first stage of temporary government outlined by the Ordinance was a simple but strongly centralized one. The Governor was clearly the dominating figure. In the second stage the people were given more power; for, although they were still subject to special laws passed by Congress for their benefit, it was a distinct gain to be allowed to elect their own representatives who were empowered to enact local laws. But the Governor still retained control of legislation by means of the veto, and he remained as before the chief power in the government.

It may be thought peculiar that the Ordinance gave the people of the Territory so few constitutional privileges. All the civil and military offices, even township and county offices, were filled by the Governor's appointment. The election of Representatives, which was the main franchise granted the people, lost much of its significance, since all legislation was subject to the Governor's absolute veto. Nor had the people any real power to act independently of the National government, since all Territorial laws were subject to the approval of Congress. But this seeming violation of recognized constitutional principles may be defended on the ground of public policy. When the original States ceded their western lands to the National government it was with the understanding that these lands would some day be carved into new States; and Congress recognized the benefit of such valuable acquisitions. But in the uncertainties of the pre-constitutional period it could by no means be predicted that the people of the rich western lands beyond the Alleghanies might not decide to shift for themselves. Hence there was need not only for a strong government, but for one which, by contrast, would offer many inducements for the early formation of States.

But it must be remembered that while the Ordinance denied the inhabitants of the Territory certain rights and privileges it also relieved them from certain duties and obligations and conferred upon them certain benefits not enjoyed by citizens in a State. On the whole the early settlers desired only freedom and protection. They were content to build homes in the wilderness, unhampered by political obligations, if only they were permitted to work out their destinies in their own way. The Ordinance was, therefore, peculiarly well adapted to frontier conditions, since it gave the settlers great freedom of action and at the same time ensured to them the largest possible measure of protection. The expenses of the Territorial government were paid out of the National treasury, as were also the cost of negotiating Indian treaties, the expense of special commissions, and the burden of maintaining the regular troops.[36] Thus the denial to the settlers of the right to participate to any great extent in the government of the Territory was offset by freedom from burdensome taxes. In addition to these facts the citizens of the Territory were to a certain degree guaranteed fair treatment from the fact that the officers were obliged to own land in the Territory and consequently had a vital interest in its welfare and prosperity.

Another important feature of the government provided by the Ordinance was that it combined the two elements of protection and of preparation for statehood. The framers of the Ordinance recognized the necessity for a course of preparation for self-government when they provided for the second stage of Territorial government.   Furthermore, statehood was held up before the people of the Territory as an incentive to progress; and they were thus assured of larger measures of self-government as rapidly as they were able to assume such responsibilities.

The Ordinance expressly provided that "There shall be formed in the said territory, not less than

three, nor more than five states'', the general boundaries of which were designated. And it was stipulated that whenever the free inhabitants of any of
these areas numbered sixty thousand they might
proceed to form a State constitution and organize
a State government.[37] It was this provision for the
admission of new States on an equality with the
original Commonwealths which marks the Ordinance
of 1787 as peculiarly unique in the history of colonial
government.

Finally, the Ordinance was more than a temporary act of legislation. For, although it was in certain respects superseded by the adoption of the
Federal Constitution,[38] the new Congress of the
United States in 1789 passed an act giving full recognition to the Ordinance, and adapting its provisions
to the new Constitution.[39] By this act it was provided that the Governor, Secretary, and Judges were
to be appointed by the President of the United
States, with the consent of the Senate — instead of
by Congress as before. The Secretary was empowered to act in the capacity of Governor in case of a
vacancy or in the Governor's absence. Except in
these merely adaptive details the Ordinance remained unchanged. It was a measure admirably
suited to the needs of a new and growing community,
and it has been used as the model for all subsequent
Territorial governments in the United States.

IV

THE ORGANIZATION OF THE TERRITORIAL
EXECUTIVE

The type of Governor provided for the Territory
by the Ordinance of 1787 was hardly one which at
first thought would be expected from the American
people.   Throughout their long experience as colonists they had been almost continually at swords
points with the Provincial Governors, resisting every
attempted exercise of arbitrary power and by means
of their legislative assemblies gradually acquiring
more and more authority at the expense of the royal
executive.[40]   But the Anglo-Saxon ideas of self-government had through centuries of growth attained a
stability that would not permit of the overthrow of
the Governor.   The people had opposed him because
of the oppressive exercise of his power and not because he was Governor.   With adequate checks and
balances he was recognized as a necessary element
in any system of government.   Consequently the
Governor, as embodying many of the characteristics
of his colonial prototype, was the natural head for
the government of the western Territories.

The question of the power of such an executive
was therefore the important consideration; and the
solution was influenced by a variety of circumstances.

As has been pointed out, when Congress was considering a form of government for the western country numerous petitions and reports revealed only too plainly the desperate and lawless condition of the frontier.   There was no restraint, no system of supervision.   The greater part of the country was an absolute wilderness, and the scattered settlements were the prey of irresponsible wanderers and Indian marauders.   Under such circumstances ordinary prudence dictated the creation of a strong government.

In the second place experience under the Articles of Confederation had already shown the dangers and impotency of a loose, decentralized form of government.   The members of the Congress of the Confederation were in a position to realize this fact most acutely; and so, it is not difficult to understand their preference for a government strongly centralized and able to act as well as to advise.

There was, moreover, another factor inhering in the very nature of the area over which the new government was to operate.   The western country was a part of the public domain which belonged to the United States.   Any form of government for such National territory must of necessity be under the supervision of the National government: it must be a branch of the parent stock and part of its policy and system.   Now the easiest and most logical method of exerting effective control over such a dependency was through a Governor appointed by the

National government. The larger the powers granted to a Governor responsible to the government above, the more effective the supervision over the dependency. Such a form of control was obviously the one best fitted to the undeveloped western country.

Still another element in determining the result was the fact that these western lands were to be settled by people from the eastern States. The settlers who were already turning their eyes westward wanted assurance that there would be a strong government able to protect them in their efforts to found homes in the western wilds. This desire is well illustrated in the petition to Congress from the Ohio Company, to which reference has already been made. The importance of the action and personal solicitation on the part of this company, perhaps, did not have as direct a bearing on shaping the form of government as is sometimes claimed for it; for the various earlier acts of the Congress relating to the West doubtless suggested many of the essentials in the final form of the Ordinance of 1787. There can be little doubt, however, but that the desire to protect the eastern settlers and encourage immigration to the West influenced the Congress of the Confederation in drawing up the mode of government. The anti-slavery clause, passed with the aid of southern men, shows how the general considerations of expediency outweighed questions of detail.

It is, of course, impossible to prove that any of these considerations resulted directly in the form of

government finally adopted. In fact it was the cumu-
lative effect of them all that shaped the legislation.
The English or American mind has never found it
difficult to frame a plan of government; and the experience and ability of the members of the Congress
of the Confederation were fully adequate to such a
task. At the same time it is scarcely possible to
escape the conclusion that these peculiar circumstances were largely instrumental in shaping a plan
of government so strongly centralized, so dominated
by one-man power, and so lacking in democratic principles as to seem repugnant to the very fundamental
ideas of self-government for which these same pa-
triots had but lately undergone all the horrors of a
revolutionary war. The evolution of such a type of
Governor, standing at the head of such a government, can only be explained by exceptional circumstances. Even though attached to a constitutional
government and safeguarded by a Bill of Rights, the
fact remains that by the Ordinance the Governor was
in reality constituted the government and the repos-
itory of political power. The wisdom of the model
as adapted to the conditions under which it was to
operate is now unquestioned, and it is evident that
the exigencies of the situation as well as a wise foresight gave rise to the provisions of the Ordinance of
1787.

The Governor provided by the Ordinance was to
be appointed by Congress, and was to hold office for
three years unless his commission was sooner re-

voked by Congress.   Thus the Governor derived his authority direct from the Federal government, and he was directly and personally responsible to it.   His commission could be revoked at any time, and hence there was an effective check upon his actions.   After the adapting act of 1789 the appointment was made by the President with the same control as before, and all reports to the government were made to the President or to his heads of departments.

Another significant provision of the Ordinance was that the Governor should reside in the district and have a freehold estate of one thousand acres of land therein while in the exercise of his office.   This was a very reasonable requirement — one intended to secure permanence in office and to reduce the probability of non-resident adventurers securing a sinecure.   It also tended to reduce absenteeism and to inspire confidence in the office because the incumbent had an actual interest in the country.

No stated salary for the Governor was stipulated in the Ordinance, but his salary was soon afterwards fixed by law at two thousand dollars per year.[41]   The law expressly provided that this amount should include compensation ''for discharging the duties of superintendent of Indian affairs in the northern department.''   In addition the sum of three hundred and fifty dollars was usually appropriated for office rent, stationery, and incidental expenses.[42]   Although the general duties of the Superintendent of Indian Affairs came within the regular salary, special ap-

propriations for negotiating Indian treaties usually
allowed the commissioners (of whom the Governor
was generally one) eight dollars per day, exclusive
of expenses during the time actually engaged.[43]
There were no other fees or emoluments connected
with the office of Governor that received official recognition, and the regular appropriation seems to
have been quite sufficient at first for the needs.

The powers given to the Governor were ample
and almost plenary in their completeness. To briefly
recapitulate, it is seen that as chief executive he was
Commander-in-Chief of the militia and appointed all
military officers below those of general rank, as well
as all civil officers except the Secretary and the three
Judges; he laid out counties and townships at his
discretion; and he had the power to call an election
for Representatives and apportion them among the
counties. He also had the usual administrative duties of a Governor to enforce the laws and preserve
the peace and security of the Territory.

Besides his executive functions the Governor, in
conjunction with the Judges, had the power to adopt
such laws as were deemed necessary for the government of the Territory. The Judges could not act
alone in this matter, and so the Governor became an
indispensable and almost controlling factor in the
legislative branch of the government. Even after
the second stage had been entered upon and a popular assembly had assumed the law-making power
the absolute veto of the Governor and his right to

convene or dissolve the assembly gave him a large control over legislation. The Governor was thus in fact the head and body of the Territorial government.

It may seem that such an extensive concentration of power in the hands of one man is little short of despotism. The judicial powers exercised by the Judges were alone of all the functions of government beyond the control of the Governor, who was responsible only to the distant and often slow-moving Federal head. But it must be remembered that the new Territory was a wild frontier land with few and scattered settlers, isolated traders and trappers, and roving bands of Indians. Here, if ever, there was need for a strong and vigorous administration — swift in action, sure in execution, and with a single, unhampered purpose. In frontier regions, as has been aptly said, "personalities counted for more than principles, and eloquence and combativeness for more than social culture and wealth." [44]   One strong, fearless man with large powers could successfully cope with the exigencies of such a situation where an intricate though model government fitted for an older community would fail utterly.

Moreover, the centering of responsibility in the Governor was commensurate with the concentration of powers. The responsibility may have been to a distant head, but it was definite and personal. The Governor alone was responsible for a just administration and for the welfare of the Territory, and this fact was bound to act as an effective check upon the too arbitrary exercise of his powers.

It is evident, therefore, that the real character of the government depended almost entirely upon the ability and personality of the Governor. If he were incompetent, dominated by selfish interests or influenced by unscrupulous advisers, the way would be open for great evil, the inevitable result of which would be oppression. If, on the other hand, he were strong and high principled, and exercised his authority solely for the best interests of the Territory, he could exert a potent influence toward building up a strong and efficient system that would be the foundation for future permanent forms of government. It is a sufficient commentary upon the wisdom of the appointments and the efficiency of the system to say that, with rare exceptions, the Territorial Governors in the United States have been able men who have builded firmly and well in founding new governments for the growing West.

The Territorial Governor presents a distinct type of executive. Although in many respects his position resembles that of the Provincial Governor of the American colonies and even approaches that of the modern European colonial Governor,[45] this western executive was, nevertheless, a peculiarly American institution erected out of definite material to meet a definite need. In organization the office of Governor was exceptionally well fitted for its purpose, and in its actual workings in the Territories of the Old Northwest it will be seen to round out into a permanent form of executive for the Territories of the United States.

V

GOVERNOR ST. CLAIR AND THE NORTH-WEST TERRITORY

On October 5, 1787, the Congress of the Confederation elected General Arthur St. Clair as the first Governor of the Territory northwest of the Ohio.[46] St. Clair was born in Scotland, of a prominent family, and was a man of wide experience and recognized ability. He had served with distinction as a soldier in both the French and Indian and the Revolutionary wars, was a staunch friend of Washington, and had been the President of the Congress of the Confederation at the time the Ordinance of 1787 was adopted. He was honest in his purposes, firm in his convictions, and unyielding in the discharge of his duty as he saw it. Jacob Burnet, a pioneer of the Old Northwest, an able lawyer, and at one time a member of the Legislative Council, has left us the following estimate of Governor St. Clair:

During the continuance of the first grade of that imperfect government, he enjoyed the respect and confidence of every class of the people. He was plain and simple in his dress and equipage, open and frank in his manners, and accessible to persons of every rank. . . . The Governor was unquestionably a man of superior talents, of extensive information, and of great uprightness of purpose, as well as suavity of manners. His general course, though in the main correct, was in some respects injurious to his own popularity; but it was the result of an honest exercise of his judgment. He not only believed that the power he claimed belonged legitimately to the executive, but was convinced that the manner in which he exercised it, was imposed upon him as a duty, by the Ordinance; and was calculated to advance the best interests of the Territory.[47]

The task of guiding the new Territory was in good hands, but the difficulties to be encountered were destined to try to the utmost the mettle of even such a sturdy character as Arthur St. Clair.

Some time was consumed by the new Governor in arranging his affairs preparatory to entering upon his administrative duties, and in the meantime the inhabitants of the western country had devised temporary expedients to preserve peace and order. Since the majority of the settlers at this time were from the Southwest the methods employed were undoubtedly those of the backwoodsman — individual vigilance and the summary visitation of punishment. But the little band of New Englanders, who in April, 1788, founded Marietta on the banks of the Ohio, with true Puritan instinct, adopted a temporary code which they publicly proclaimed by tacking it upon a tree and selecting one of their number to enforce its provisions.[48] A traveler who journeyed down the Ohio recorded in his journal that many needed regulations for the government of the new colony were read, militia officers named, and provisions for guard and military duty drawn up.[49]

On July 9, 1788, Governor St. Clair arrived at Marietta and was welcomed by a salute of fourteen guns and other evidences of general rejoicing. Six days later, with impressive inaugural ceremonies, he was installed in office.[50]

The local makeshifts at government which St. Clair found upon his arrival in the Territory only served to emphasize the need of careful organization, and to call attention more strongly to the vast regions without a vestige of legal supervision or control. The establishment of the necessary machinery for local government was therefore one of the first tasks to be undertaken. The Ordinance furnished the fundamental framework, but the institutional details had to be constructed out of the available material.

On July 27, 1788, the Governor issued a proclamation establishing the County of Washington, which embraced within its limits all of the settled portions of the Territory.[51] He also appointed the necessary sheriffs, clerks of court, judges of probate, justices of the peace, coroners, and some lesser civil officers, as well as the required military officers. The duties of these officials were very general at first and without jurisdictional qualifications. In fact the scattered settlements were compelled to look after their own interests more or less for a time. The County of Washington seems to have been erected mainly as a basis of organization until laws could be passed and a more complete system put into operation.

The Governor had scarcely assumed the duties of his office before he received from two of the Judges the draft of a law providing for the organization of the militia. St. Clair, being a soldier, at once saw the defects in the proposed organization, which was more theoretical than practical; and, moreover, he thought he perceived an undue assumption of the initiative on the part of the Judges. So the draft was returned with recommendations for a more practical system, which were soon embodied in the first law of the new Territory.[52]

Before the end of the year 1788 the Governor and the Judges, acting together as the law-making body, passed ten laws to meet the most pressing needs of the Territory.[53] Four years later one of these laws which had considerably shortened the time in which actions at law could be brought, was disapproved of by Congress.[54] The law was evidently regarded as too radical a departure from the recognized legal standard of a statute of limitation, although it may have been founded on sound policy in respect to conditions as they existed in the Territory. The law respecting crimes and punishments was also later repealed and a substitute law was enacted to meet the need of changed conditions.[55] With these two exceptions the ten statutes were later confirmed by the Territorial legislature and embodied in the code, thus indicating the permanent fitness of these early enactments.

Officers having been appointed and laws promulgated, the next step in the organization of the government was the establishment of a system of courts. Accordingly, on September 2, 1788, with appropriate ceremonies, the judiciary was formally inaugurated.[56]

The judicial system had evidently been carefully planned, and it was surprisingly comprehensive for a new country. The three Judges, appointed by the President of the United States, sitting together formed the Supreme Court, which had a general Territorial and appellate jurisdiction and convened whenever and wherever the three members could come together. The court of common pleas was an inferior court having a general common law jurisdiction, though concurrent in the various counties with the jurisdiction of the Supreme Court, and was made up of not less than three nor more than seven appointive judges. The general quarter sessions of the peace was a still lower court with a limited criminal jurisdiction, and was composed of a number of justices in each county.[57]

The judges and justices of the two lower courts were also given certain civil and criminal powers that could be exercised individually outside of the regular court. This provision afforded better protection to the people and facilitated the ordinary business of the courts. Justice was not dependent upon the periodical sittings of the courts, but became more swift and sure at all times — a very necessary precaution in a frontier country. The pioneer judges may have been ignorant of many of the forms of law, but they seem to have been able to dispense the kind of frontier justice that was best suited to the particular case in hand.[58]   Law and justice are fundamental to the growth and prosperity of any community, and the early establishment of a sound and progressive judicial policy contributed in a large measure to the success of Territorial government in the Old Northwest.

In 1790 the counties of Knox, St. Clair, and Hamilton were established in the same manner as the County of Washington.[59]   The necessary officers were appointed and their respective jurisdictions were somewhat more carefully defined than before. At the same time the local government was further developed by the organization of civil townships. The Governor and Judges passed a law requiring the justices of the court of quarter sessions to divide each county into townships with such boundaries as they should deem proper.   They were to appoint for each of such townships a constable to act "specially" for the township and "generally" for the county, and also a clerk and one or more overseers of the poor.[60]

The system of local government thus established indicates the predominance of southern and middle Atlantic State influences rather than the town meet-

ing tendency of the New England States. In fact the
system so closely resembled that of Pennsylvania
that it is probable that St. Clair, who was himself a
Pennsylvanian, was largely instrumental in framing
it. If this is true it affords an interesting example
of the influence of the Governor in practical matters.

In 1802, responding to the desire for a more
democratic local government, a further step in the
evolution of the characteristic western county-town-
ship system was taken. In that year the Territorial
legislature passed an act establishing the township
meeting for elections, creating several new offices,
and making some alterations in the duties of the various officers.[61] The local government in the Territories and States formed out of the Old Northwest
after 1802 may, therefore, be said to be the result of
sectional compromise, since it combined the county
system of the southern and middle States with elements of the town meeting idea of New England.

There are many inherent difficulties connected
with the establishment of a new government in a new
country. But the task of Governor St. Clair became
doubly difficult, for, from the beginning, he had to
contend against inharmonious elements within the
inner circles of the governmental organization itself.

The Judges were sensitive about their rights in
the making of laws, and at times were inclined to
resent the vigorous and practical manner in which
St. Clair shared in the first attempts at legislation.
Shortly after the rebuff in regard to the organization

of the militia St. Clair declined to give his assent to
a law establishing probate offices in the Territory,
thereby arousing the displeasure of the Judges. In
a letter replying to Governor St. Clair, Judges Parsons and Varnum, by a veiled reference, attempted
to interpret the clause of the Ordinance which provided that the "governor and judges, or a majority
of them," should adopt laws for the Territory as
meaning that the Judges could act in that capacity
without the Governor. "The exercise [of legal dis-
cretion]", they said, "is checked by the tenures of
our commissions, the necessity that the governor and
two of the judges, or that all the judges, must agree,
and the final negative of Congress." [62]

The Governor, however, by a reply as vigorous
as it was unanswerable, nipped in the bud this attempt to undermine his prerogative. "I conceive,
gentlemen", he wrote, "Congress thought there
would be an impropriety in leaving the adoption of
laws by which the people of the district were for a
time to be governed solely to the persons who were
to expound them; much greater, however, would that
impropriety be if the clause of the Ordinance goes
not only to adoption, but to the formation of laws.
The judges would in that case be complete legislators, which is the very definition of tyranny; and
though that arrangement might in your hands, gentlemen, produce no evils, no man can tell how long
this stage of the government will last, or who may
be your successors; nor could it fail to produce much

uneasiness in the minds of the people over whom so, possibly, oppressive an authority was established."[63] It was fortunate that St. Clair maintained this position so tenaciously, for his sound common sense formed a balance-wheel that regulated and controlled the often erratic proposals of the Judges.

As a matter of fact, while some of the Judges were able men, they often went to extremes in their efforts to counteract the influence of the Governor's decisive personality; and some of them were exceedingly narrow and prejudiced. For instance, Judge John Cleves Symmes had secured extensive grants from the government and owned vast tracts of land in the Territory while on the bench,[64] and he was from the first unfriendly to the Governor. In writing to St. Clair in 1791 in reply to a letter from the Governor, Symmes spoke of "harsh sentences, mortifying expressions and implied reflections therein used"; and after further criticism closed by saying: "It is no longer necessary that the man who rises to power should mount his pegasus, by setting his foot on the neck of him who is not quite so tall as himself."[65] And from time to time the acts of St. Clair called for his vituperative condemnation, until at last after a bitter indictment he boldly called upon the Governor to resign.[66]

While St. Clair was vigorous in what he said and did, he was at all times dignified and courteous; and making allowances for contemporary partisanship and prejudice, it is generally considered that he endeavored to be fair to his opponents as well as to his friends. That he was not intolerant or unreasonably obstinate in holding to his own views is shown in another difference of opinion between him and the Judges. The clause of the Ordinance of 1787 which related to the law-making power provided that the "governor and judges . . . . shall adopt and publish in the district, such laws of the original states, criminal and civil, as may be necessary". This clause plainly gave the Governor and Judges no authority to enact laws *de novo,* but only the power to select such statutes as had previously been passed by the older States. It is probable that this provision was intended as a check upon the legislators by confining them to laws approved by experience, thus being an additional precaution against unwise legislation.

In actual practice, however, this clause seriously hampered the Governor and Judges, since it was very difficult to find laws of the States that were applicable to the peculiar conditions in the Territory. And so the Judges proceeded to construe the power to adopt laws into authority to enact new ones; and a majority of the Territorial laws before 1795 were enacted in accordance with this interpretation. Governor St. Clair acquiesced in this practice with great reluctance, as he realized that it was stretching the plain limits of the legislative authority granted by the Ordinance.[67] But the manifest necessity of the occasion led him to defer to the Judges and to what

he felt would be for the best interests of the Territory.

The attitude of Congress toward these early
Territorial laws was one of indifference. The Ordinance provided that the laws were to remain in force
unless disapproved of by Congress. But in reality
Congress was indifferent until especially urged to
action.   Resolutions were occasionally passed by
one house of Congress or the other disapproving of
certain Territorial laws. One joint resolution to
the same effect was introduced, but it was not adopted by the Senate, it is said, because the members accepted St. Clair's view that not having been adopted
in accordance with the Ordinance the laws were *ipso
facto* void and it was therefore not necessary to declare them so.[68] In fact only one law was disapproved of by Congress.[69] The other laws, having
been adopted and published in the Territory, were
considered valid, even though technically defective
in the manner of their enactment; and they were so
necessary to the welfare of the Territory that they
were regularly enforced until they later received the
proper sanction of the Territorial legislature.[70]

It was only in the enactment of the earliest laws
of the Territory, however, that this broad interpretation of the provision of the Ordinance was put into
practice. In the *Maxwell Code,* which contains the
laws for the year 1795, the statutes of the original
States from which the laws were taken are in each
case indicated in the heading. It is a significant fact

that of the thirty-seven laws which thus express their
source, twenty-five were taken from Pennsylvania,
six from Massachusetts, three from Virginia, one
from New York, one from New Jersey, and one from
Pennsylvania and New York.[71] This predominance
of Pennsylvania statutes may have been partly due
to the fact that, because of somewhat similar conditions, the laws of Pennsylvania were especially well
suited for the western country. But it is also doubtless true that St. Clair was so strongly imbued with
the legal system and the institutions of Pennsylvania, that he impressed them strongly upon the new
Territory. Such facts as these afford an insight
into the molding influences at work in the Old Northwest, and also point out the real power of the Territorial Governor.

In dealing with the differences between the
branches of his government St. Clair, in his characteristic way, used force rather than tact. Instead
of overcoming opposition, he kept it continually
stirred up; and so he was always forced to contend
against adverse elements in outlining Territorial
policies and in carrying them into effect.

But the formation and administration of a work-
ing government on the plan outlined in the Ordinance was not the only task that confronted the new
Governor. The Territory was so surrounded and
honeycombed by conflicting interests that it was indeed in a precarious situation. A less fearless and

self-confident man than St. Clair would have been appalled at the prospect.

In the first place, the needs of the settlers demanded attention. As nearly as can be determined there were less than seven thousand white people in the Territory at the time of its organization, and they were scattered over many hundred miles of wilderness.[72]   The Americans were comparatively few and widely scattered, and consisted of a heterogenous class of emigrants from many different States, clustered in small settlements at the most favorable locations along the banks of the rivers. But more people were constantly coming, and particularly during the first few summers settlers began to pour into the Ohio country. Many of these newcomers, especially the old Revolutionary soldiers, were indigent or ill-prepared to withstand the rigors of an extreme winter, and consequently they often suffered the greatest hardships and privations. The French inhabitants at the old posts on the Wabash and Mississippi rivers were also often in destitute circumstances.

With few resources at his command St. Clair put forth his best efforts to relieve this distress, and during the first years of his administration the calls upon him for relief formed an important element in the problems of government, as well as imposing a great personal burden upon the Governor himself. ''He made repeated journeys'', says his biographer, ''from one part of the Territory to another, sleeping upon the ground or in an open boat, and living upon coarse and uncertain fare. At one time he traveled in this manner a distance of five thousand miles, without the means of protection against inclement weather, and without rest.''[73]

In the second place, the various foreign settlements within the Territory and on its borders formed a disturbing element. The settlements of French and Creoles, mainly at Vincennes, Kaskaskia, and the Illinois villages, together with the French traders and trappers, were difficult to handle. Accustomed as these people were to the French system of government, and unable to comprehend or appreciate American ideas or to carry out the small measure of self-government provided for them, the task of government became a very puzzling one. The Governor was obliged to translate all the laws and notices for their benefit;[74] and even then the easy-going Frenchmen were often indifferent in their obedience. As General Harmar had said, they were fitted only for a commandant and a military domination.[75] They were, indeed, very much like wayward children and required about as much attention.

The Spaniards across the Mississippi were another and even greater menace to the Territory. Alien by blood and temperament, with a blind devotion to Spain and her interests, they were intensely jealous of any encroachment that would tend to control the Mississippi or imperil the Spanish territory of Louisiana; and as a consequence they hampered the movements of the Americans in every possible manner. The story of their intrigues and desperate attempts to hold their colonies in the new world is well known, and it must be apparent that they were undesirable neighbors for the new and ambitious Territory northwest of the Ohio.[76]

Embittered by the loss of territory that followed the Revolution, the English on the northern border were also covertly hostile. They realized that the westward advancement of the Americans was undermining their monopoly of the fur trade and would soon open up a ready outlet to the south that would divert the bulk of the furs and skins from their northern trading posts. Accordingly, they held on to Detroit and the northern frontier long after they should have been relinquished. Thus, for years Detroit remained a hotbed from which emanated evil influences that menaced the prosperity of the Northwest Territory.[77] And not the least among these baneful influences was the practice of inciting the Indians to keep up a constant border warfare against the Americans.[78]

Again, the Public Domain itself was a source of considerable trouble. Innumerable grants of land had been made in this region by the French and the English governments, and after the establishment of American rule the civil courts and the successors of John Todd had also assumed the right to make land grants. The result was many confusing and conflicting claims and a constant contention among the settlers. The French, especially, seldom knew whether they had any title to their lands or not; and they were constantly appealing to the Governor for aid. Many settlers had also staked out claims which could not be reconciled with those of their neighbors, and so conflicts concerning boundaries very frequently arose. St. Clair was instructed to adjust these matters, and he devoted much time to the endeavor to straighten out the many difficulties which had arisen. But finally he reported that in a great number of cases the claims were irreconcilable and recommended the right of preëmption for actual settlers.[79]

Another difficulty was that neighboring States often pursued policies that interfered with Territorial business, and often their selfish indifference or refusal to coöperate worked great injury to the Territory.[80]

Finally, the Indians were without doubt the greatest menace to the safety of the settlers and to the successful administration of the government of the Territory. With growing hostility the Indians saw the white settlers flocking across the Ohio, which they considered as the natural boundary of their hunting grounds. Urged on by the intimations and presents of English agents and traders, they became more and more treacherous until at last the conflict with the settlers became a relentless, bloody warfare. The lonely settler in his cabin or the dweller in the stronghold of the settlement were alike in danger;

for the savage, silent as the night and implacable in
his murderous desires, would strike in an unguarded
moment and carry off in triumph the bloody scalps
of his victims.   The life of the isolated settler became a constant nightmare of fear, and many times
Indian war parties spread terror, anguish, and desolation throughout the Territory.

Among the first communications received by
Governor St. Clair from the National government
was one which contained secret instructions regarding the conduct of Indian affairs,[81] and a perusal of
the Governor's correspondence will reveal the fact
that dealings with the Indians engrossed the greater
part of his time and attention.[82] He held councils
and negotiated treaties with the friendly tribes, and
often personally conducted expeditions and campaigns against hostile and depredating bands of Indians.   But his resources were entirely inadequate
to cope successfully with the situation, and his appeals for aid met with but feeble response from the
National government.   The troops at his command
consisted of a few regulars assisted by the Territorial militia. St. Clair was not sufficiently popular to
secure the confidence of his troops, and hence was
not able to make the most of such forces as were at
his command.   Furthermore, he was a colonial soldier trained in the school of regular warfare and he
did not fully understand or sympathize with the
western methods of fighting.   As a result his campaigns were by no means universally successful.

Finally, in November, 1791, while encamped on a branch of the Wabash River his small army was attacked and mowed down by the hidden savages in a slaughter that stands second only to Braddock's defeat in a previous war. The Governor, fatigued by continual exertion and weakened by sickness, was almost incapable of commanding at such a critical moment, but he bravely remained at his post. "St. Clair, with his gray hair streaming under his cocked hat, had horse after horse shot under him as he endeavored to make his force stand steady amid the frightful carnage. He had eight bullets pierce his garments, but not one grazed his skin."[83] But all his endeavors were in vain, for incompetence had undermined the efficiency of the army. St. Clair undoubtedly showed lack of foresight and poor generalship in planning the campaign and in allowing himself to be trapped; but the consensus of opinion now seems to be that it was mismanagement and lack of support on the part of the general government that formed the fundamental cause of this crushing defeat.[84]

The people of the whole country were greatly wrought up over this unexpected disaster, and the National government was also awakened to a realization of the seriousness of the situation.[85] Congress immediately authorized the raising of troops, which, drilled and led by General Anthony Wayne, soon broke the Indian resistance and secured comparative peace for the Territory.

It was amid such trying conditions as these that the work of governing the Territory was carried on. It should not be forgotten that this was the first government of its kind and that Governor St. Clair had few precedents to guide him. The inherent difficulties and the external dangers combined to make the task an unusually difficult one. The way, however, was not everywhere beset with obstacles, and much was accomplished in the ordinary course of administration.

Strange as it may seem, the Ordinance of 1787 made no provision for the repeal of laws adopted by the Governor and Judges during the first stage of Territorial government. The laws were to remain in force until the organization of the legislature ''unless disapproved of by Congress'', regardless of whether in practice they had become obsolete or not, or even if conditions had so changed as to render such laws oppressive. St. Clair called attention to this evil, and in 1792 Congress passed an act giving the Governor and Judges the authority to repeal laws as well as to make them.[86] This necessary adjunct to the law-making power was exercised with good results, especially at the time of the codification of the laws.

Another cause of complaint among certain classes of the inhabitants of the Territory was the difficulty of convening the Supreme Court. The country was still an untamed wilderness and the uncertainties of travel from one sitting to another were so pronounced that two Judges could seldom get together without great expense and hardship.[87] So Congress, in the act of 1792 just referred to, empowered a single Judge to hold court without appeal.[88] St. Clair opposed this measure as impolitic — for the very cogent reasons that it gave one Judge absolute legal power, and that two of the Judges had large landed interests upon which they could not fairly sit in judgment and which might tend, though unconsciously, to influence their adjudication if acting alone. On these grounds he very strongly advised the repeal of the measure.[89] Congress later reconsidered the ill-advised law, and in accordance with St. Clair's suggestion it was repealed.

After the adoption of the first ten laws, the Governor and Judges continued to enact statutes covering practically the whole range of jurisprudence. St. Clair had for some time cherished a desire to revise and codify these laws; and so in 1795 the codification was begun by the Governor and Judges. The work was done systematically and with the idea of conforming to the provisions of the Ordinance as well as of securing a complete code. The judicial system was altered in certain respects. The sittings of the Supreme Court were fixed at Marietta and Cincinnati; circuit courts were established to facilitate the trial of higher cases; and orphan courts were instituted for the purpose of enlarging the powers of the probate judges.[90] As an addition to the principles of the Common Law a statute was enacted

at this time providing equitable remedies in certain
cases. This law was adopted from the statutes of
Massachusetts and was the beginning of equity procedure in the Territory.[91]

The most noticeable feature of the laws thus
codified is the criminal code.[92] At that time (and
indeed until long afterward) the old barbaric modes
of punishment were still employed in the eastern
States. And so, naturally, they were adopted in the
Northwest Territory, where there may have been
more necessity for such summary measures owing
to the lack of prisons and the machinery for prosecution. At any rate the death penalty was provided
for murder and treason, and for arson if accompanied by loss of life. Perjury was punishable by
a fine of not over sixty dollars, or by whipping not
to exceed thirty-nine stripes and sitting in the pillory
not over two hours; but the culprit was also declared
forever incapable of holding office, giving testimony,
or serving as a juror. For obstructing an officer of
the law the offender was to receive not to exceed
thirty-nine lashes, and be fined not more than three
hundred dollars. Larceny was punished by requiring restitution of double the value of the article
stolen, with a fine or thirty-nine stripes at the discretion of the court. Drunkenness was punishable
by a fine, the non-payment of which consigned the
offender to the stocks. Various other crimes and
offences were punished proportionately. Imprisonment for debt was also especially provided for by

law.[93] These measures seem harsh to-day, but they
were in harmony with the spirit of the time.

The general system of law contained in the code
was fairly representative; but as a final and comprehensive measure, there was added a statute which
provided that the Common Law of England prior to
the fourth year of the reign of James I should be in
full force within the Territory.[94] It would perhaps
have been difficult to define just what the Common
Law of England was during the period named, but to
a legal mind it conveyed a very definite idea; and
thus in a substantial manner the law served a useful
purpose, even though by the Ordinance the course
of the Common Law in judicial proceedings had
already been guaranteed to the people of the Territory. It could hardly be expected that a new code
in a new country would be sufficiently ample to meet
the needs of all future adjudications; and so in a
contingency where none of the laws of the code were
applicable, and without any reported cases to serve
as precedents, justice might easily be defeated unless there was something to fall back upon. But
with the general principles of the Common Law in
reserve, the Judges could without difficulty decide
justly and impartially all cases which came before
them. The result of the codification was on the
whole very satisfactory, and it gave to the Territory a definite body of laws.

When ten years under the first stage of government had passed, the population had so increased

that the Territory was entitled to enter upon the second stage provided for in the Ordinance. Pursuant to the call of the Governor in 1798 Representatives were elected, and in the following year they assembled and chose ten Councilmen from whom the President of the United States selected five.[95] On September 16, 1799, the first Territorial legislature of the Old Northwest convened at Cincinnati.

Governor St. Clair was now confronted by another element opposing his administrative policy. While it is doubtless true that the first legislature contained many men of considerable ability, and that the laws enacted were in the main salutary, nevertheless some of the enactments were certainly open to question. The legislature, all powerful in its own eyes, undertook a rather comprehensive scheme of laying out new counties which met with the disapproval of the Governor. And so, in a speech terminating the protracted session, he vetoed absolutely eleven acts, six of which related to the erection of new counties. "It appears to me", said St. Clair, "that the erecting of new counties is the proper business of the Executive. It is, indeed, provided that the boundaries of counties may be altered by the legislature; but that is quite a different thing from originally establishing them. They must exist before they can be altered, and the provision is express that the Governor shall proceed, from time to time, as it may become necessary to lay them out.

While I shall ever most studiously avoid encroaching on any of the rights of the legislature, you will naturally expect, gentlemen, that I should guard with equal care those of the Executive.''[96]

This free use of the veto power caused much dissatisfaction among the people and precipitated an extended controversy with the legislature. There seems to have been some sort of a political scheme in this proposed districting of the Territory, and the legislators were in reality as much angered because of the frustration of their pet plans as they appeared to be over the alleged abuse of the veto power. They had attempted a species of what in modern parlance would be termed ''gerrymandering''. But there were also outside influences at work, and as one writer points out, much of the bitterness of the controversy was ''due to land-speculators, anxious to influence the erection of counties and the location of county towns, who found Governor St. Clair standing in their way.''[97]

It is not surprising, therefore, that St. Clair became very unpopular and that his relations with the legislature grew more and more bitter. Memorials were addressed to Congress, and there were numerous popular complaints, but the Governor entirely ignored them all. Throughout the struggle with the legislature — which lasted until the end of the Territorial government — St. Clair never wavered from the straight line of duty as he saw it. He may have drawn the line more strictly because of the opposi-

tion to him, but it was still his duty to the Territory
as it appeared to him.   Thus he continually thwarted
the machinations of the designing or the unscrupulous, and also prevented the passage of much unwise, though well intended legislation.   He may have
used the veto power with considerable freedom, but
it was a precaution on the side of safety which on
the whole undoubtedly resulted beneficially for the
Territory.

In spite of his fearless devotion to duty, it must
be admitted that in many ways St. Clair was unfortunate in his attitude toward the people over whom
he was placed.   He was a staunch Federalist, while
the people of the Territory were ardent Republicans,
and this fact opened a breach which his eastern in-
clinations and his entire failure to appreciate the
frontiersman widened still further.   The autocratic
tendencies of St. Clair were incompatible with western independence and democracy; and it is probable
that his vigorous administration would have aroused
violent opposition long before it did if it had not
been tempered with dignity and impartiality.   As
it was the conflict gradually became more intense
until the final split came on the question of the formation of a State government for the eastern part of
the Territory.

St. Clair opposed the movement for statehood,
and a bitter controversy followed.   Indignation
against the Governor ran so high at Chillicothe that
on two successive evenings the mob insulted the Gov-

ernor until he finally adjourned the legislature to Cincinnati, thus removing the seat of government to the latter place.[98] The Territory was torn with dissension, but in the end the advocates of statehood triumphed.

While the first convention to form a State constitution was in session, St. Clair sent word that as Governor he would address the convention. A resolution that he should be heard was voted down, but in another resolution the members of the convention announced their willingness to listen to Arthur St. Clair, Sr., Esq., if he wished to speak.[99] This direct rebuff was too much even for the self-contained St. Clair, and he launched forth in a speech which it must be admitted somewhat overstepped the bounds of dignity and propriety. The result was a severe rebuke from the President of the United States, accompanied by a summary dismissal from the governorship.[100] "Thomas Jefferson would have shown himself a larger man", is Professor Hinsdale's comment, "if he had overlooked the indiscretion of the Chillicothe speech and permitted the venerable Governor to remain at the head of the Territory the few weeks yet to elapse before it ceased to exist."[101]

It was, indeed, an unfortunate ending to the public career of Arthur St. Clair. He had rendered faithful service to his country and had given his best and most mature years to the building up of the Territory with which his name will always be associated. His strict honesty prevented him from making money either by virtue of his office or by speculation in land, and after leaving the office of Governor he lived in poverty and almost hermit-like retirement. Some years later he died, unnoticed and unmourned by a forgetful government and an ungrateful people.

Thus closed the history of the Northwest Territory. In 1802 the eastern part of the Territory was admitted into the Union as the State of Ohio.[102] The result of the Territorial strife between the legislature and the Governor found expression in the Constitution of the new State. In its reaction against one-man power, it stripped the governorship of many of its usual powers and duties, so that the Governor became merely a figure-head with a few unimportant functions.[103]

It was peculiarly fortunate that the system of Territorial government in the United States was at the beginning guided by so able and steadfast a Governor as Arthur St. Clair. The signal success of the initial trial in the Northwest Territory must in a large measure be ascribed to him.

VI

GOVERNOR HARRISON AND THE INDIANA TERRITORY

The Northwest Territory was divided by an act of Congress of May 7, 1800; and all that part lying west of a line beginning at the Ohio opposite the mouth of the Kentucky River, and running thence to Fort Recovery, and thence north to the Canadian border, was called Indiana Territory.[104] The reason for this division is to be found in the fact that Congress desired to admit Ohio into the Union as soon as possible; and since the eastern portion of the Territory had grown very rapidly in population this desire might soon be fulfilled. Moreover, it was becoming increasingly difficult to govern the older part of the Territory on an equal basis with the large western region, which was still for the most part a wilderness with only a few scattered settlements. In 1800, according to the census, there were only four thousand eight hundred and seventy-five people, exclusive of Indians; in the country included in the new Territory, and they were located chiefly at or in the vicinity of the villages of Vincennes, Kaskaskia, and Cahokia. Courts in these outlying regions were held at irregular intervals; while administration from a distance invited many demoralizing tendencies.[105]

The act of Congress provided that the government of the Indiana Territory should be in all respects similar to that outlined in the Ordinance of 1787, and that the inhabitants should enjoy all the rights and advantages secured to the people by that instrument. The same powers and duties were assigned to the officers and they were to receive the same emoluments as were given to similar officers in the Northwest Territory. By thus providing for a government similar to that of the older Territory the Ordinance practically transferred to the Territory of Indiana a government ready made. St. Clair had worked out many of the most difficult problems of administration, and the new Territory inherited the results of his labors and experience.

The fourth section of the Organic Act of the Indiana Territory made the further provision that the part of the Ordinance of 1787 which referred to the organization of a general assembly should become operative whenever it was shown to the Governor that a majority of the freeholders desired such an assembly, regardless of whether the Territory had five thousand free male inhabitants or not. The people of the Indiana country, while included within the bounds and jurisdiction of the Northwest Territory, had borne their share of the trials of preparation for self-government. Many of the settlements, though more widely scattered, were nearly as far advanced as the eastern portion of the Old Northwest. Consequently it would have been a needless waste of time, as well as an unwarrantable aggravation, to have placed the inhabitants of the western region back in the initial stages of the Territorial system. The privilege of electing a general assembly upon the demand of a majority of the voters without the necessity of waiting for a large increase in population was a distinct step in advance.

Under these favorable circumstances the government of the Indiana Territory was organized with William Henry Harrison as Governor.   Harrison was a man well fitted for the position.   He was a product of the West, and was thoroughly in sympathy with western ideas and institutions.   He had served with distinction under St. Clair and Wayne and was well trained in the methods of Indian warfare.   As Secretary of the Northwest Territory toward the latter part of St. Clair's administration, and as Delegate to Congress from that Territory, Harrison had gained much valuable experience in the management of Territorial affairs.   Energetic and courageous and at the same time prudent in his undertakings, he resembled St. Clair in the strict honesty with which he administered the duties of his office.[106]

While a Delegate to Congress Harrison had secured the passage of an act permitting the sale of government land in small subdivisions (instead of in tracts of four thousand acres as before), thus giving the individual settler an opportunity to buy directly from the government, instead of through land

companies.[107]   This service was warmly appreciated
by the western settlers and it gained popularity for
Harrison throughout the West. In spite of the somewhat dictatorial powers which he possessed as Governor of the Indiana Territory, and the consequent
difficulty of pleasing everyone, he retained the good
will of the people to a great extent during his entire
administration.

The task of organizing the new Territory was
not a difficult one, since the Governor and Judges
were not obliged to formulate and enact a new set of
fundamental laws, but could make use of the Code
already in force in the Northwest Territory. Instead
of being hampered at the outset, as St. Clair had
been, by the necessity of adopting all their laws from
the statutes of the original thirteen States, they had
the advantage of a complete body of laws ready to be
applied to the administration of the new Territory.
The code of laws adopted by the Governor and
Judges of the Northwest Territory was not formally
reënacted, the assumption being that the division of
the Territory was simply to facilitate administration
and that, therefore, the laws remained in force in
both sections the same as though there had been no
division. Hence it was that the first legislative acts
of the Governor and Judges of the Indiana Territory, passed at their first meeting at Point Vincennes
on January 12, 1801, were laws supplemental to or
repealing certain laws previously enacted in the
Northwest Territory.[108]

Whenever new laws were adopted in the Indiana Territory the usual form of indicating the statute of the original State from which the law was taken, as required by the Ordinance, was generally employed, although the custom continued to hamper the Governor and Judges in their work. This fact is illustrated by a resolution relative to ferries. The resolution stated that the law at that time provided for application to the legislature for permission to establish ferries, but since no legislature had yet been organized in the Territory, and no laws on the subject of ferries could be found except such as were of a purely local nature, the Governor was empowered to establish such ferries by proclamation.[109]

It is a significant fact that the Governor and Judges of the Indiana Territory took the majority of their laws from the statutes of southern States. Of those laws in which reference was made to the States from which they were taken, seven were from Virginia; three from Kentucky; two from Virginia and Kentucky; one from New York, Pennsylvania and Virginia; one from Virginia and Pennsylvania; and two from Pennsylvania.[110] Governor Harrison was a Virginian by birth and early training, and this fact is doubtless a partial explanation of the predominance of Virginia statutes adopted during the first years of Territorial government in Indiana.

The fact that the Code of the Northwest Territory was employed in the Indiana Territory would probably not have occasioned any inconvenience had not Governor Harrison and the Judges passed several laws modifying judicial procedure to meet the requirements of the new country.[111]   These changes gave rise to complications by affording opportunity for a clash of jurisdictions.   Mr. Dunn cites an interesting example of such conflict in a case which came before the Territorial court in 1803. The question was one concerning a law regulating prison bounds; and the court held that a law passed in the Northwest Territory, even after 1800 when Indiana was set off by itself, was still in force in Wayne County, which had been added to the Indiana Territory in 1802, notwithstanding the fact that an entirely different law was in force in the remainder of Indiana.[112]   Thus the prisoner incarcerated under the old law was still amenable thereto, although his jailor was enforcing a different law.   It is apparent that confusion would necessarily result from such a duality of laws.

Evidently the amendments and adaptations of the original Code were made without proper care to harmonize the new provisions with the general tenor of the laws themselves, and this process of incongruous grafting and unwise pruning played havoc with the judicial system of the Indiana Territory.[113] Consequently the use of the completed Code of the Northwest Territory, which at first was such an advantage to the new government, later became the very means of producing irregularity.   The evil was partially remedied by an act of Congress in 1815;[114]

and the formation of a State government for the
Commonwealth of Indiana in the following year
gave an opportunity for the establishment of a system consonant with experience.

The confusion, however, was confined to the
organization and work of the judicial department.
In the meantime the administration of the government was being ably conducted by Governor Harrison, and the rugged persistence and ability displayed
during his later career revealed themselves in his
actions during these years. He did not too highly
esteem the mere powers of the office, as St. Clair had
done; nor did he so punctiliously guard its prerogatives from intrenchment. By keeping in close touch
with the people he avoided much of the trouble and
controversy which St. Clair had undergone.

The system of local government having been
well organized by the Governor and Judges and
legislature of the Northwest Territory, the county
officers were in the main continued; and thus the
transition from one jurisdiction to another was
achieved with scarcely an incident to disturb the ef-
fectiveness of the system. There was no necessity
for transplanting the local system of the Northwest
Territory, for it continued to grow in the same soil
and under practically the same conditions.   Thus,
with many precedents to guide him, with much of the
internal organization already arranged by the Code
of the Northwest Territory, and with laws provided
from the same source, Governor Harrison had much

more time for the direction of external relations, especially for the conduct of Indian affairs.

The act which created the Indiana Territory expressly provided that the duties and emoluments of Superintendent of Indian Affairs should be united with those of Governor. But the National government, recognizing the importance of the work, appointed Governor Harrison special and sole commissioner to treat with the northwestern tribes, with secret powers and with instructions to draw any money he might think necessary to accomplish the objects entrusted to him.[115]   Under this power he negotiated with remarkable success fourteen treaties with the Indians[116] and extinguished the Indian title to millions of acres of land at a very small cost.[117]

These Indian cessions were of great importance as they opened up large tracts of land for settlement, and, as Jefferson pointed out in his message to Congress, were of "strategic value in case of war", because "every new purchase of Indian lands was equivalent to providing a new army" for the protection of settlers and for reducing the hostile country.[118]   Indeed, the relations with the Indians engaged the greater share of Governor Harrison's time and attention, and he was almost constantly busied in conducting expeditions, making treaties, purchasing land, or acting as mediator in settling the troublesome differences between the tribes.[119] The task of maintaining peace among the warlike savages was a very exacting and delicate one, and

the efficiency with which he discharged this often
onerous and dangerous duty and the ability with
which he conducted his Indian campaigns gave Harrison a National reputation.

Another duty which at first bore heavily upon
Governor Harrison was the settlement of the many
questions concerning conflicting claims and titles to
the public lands.   Harrison fell heir to most of the
difficulties which St. Clair had experienced with these
same questions.[120]   The Governor had the power to
confirm grants already made, but a careful investigation was necessary to guard against fraud.   The
adjustment of claims was of necessity so slow, and
fraud and imposition were so generally practiced
upon the Governor, that in 1804 Congress passed a
sweeping law establishing land offices at Detroit,
Vincennes, and Kaskaskia, and appointing a Register
and a Receiver of Public Moneys for each.[121]   This
act required all claimants to land by virtue of any
grant from the French, British, or United States
governments to record their claims in the proper
land office, or upon failure to do so they would be
forever barred from claiming any right thereto. The
Registers and Receivers were appointed commissioners to examine claims, receive evidence, and ''decide
thereon according to justice and equity'', and they
were to submit their decisions to Congress for final
approval.[122]

The establishment of land offices systematized
the process of establishing claims and provided a

regular machinery for effectively dealing with dis-
putes. Settlements and adjustments could be accomplished much more expeditiously than by the
overworked Governor. But even the Commissioners, with added powers, found the task a difficult one,
and their report in 1810 expressed much discourage-
ment.[123]

Acting on this report the committee of the House
of Representatives, which had under consideration
the land claims in the District of Kaskaskia, recommended that the Governor's decisions should be re-
examined. "It ought to be remarked," stated the
report of the committee, "to show the necessity of a
re-examination of these claims, as well as to do
justice to the Governors who made the confirmations,
that the multifarious duties imposed on these officers,
in their capacity of Governor, Indian agent, and, in
one instance, of commander-in-chief, did not allow
them the time necessary for the full investigation of
the claims presented for their decision; and, perhaps,
unsuspicious of the practices of fraud, forgery, and
perjury that have been since developed by the investigation of the commissioners, they may not have
examined the claims with that scrupulous attention
that was necessary to guard the public property
against impositions."[124]

These recommendations were, however, not then
acted upon by Congress; and it is interesting to note
that in 1830 a committee of the Senate advised the
acceptance of the Governor's grants in certain cases,

on the ground that they were based upon better evidence than could at that time be procured by the
commissioners.[125] At all events it was almost impossible to reconcile the conflicting claims and grants,
and although the new Commissioners may have un-
covered more fraud and chicanery than the Governor
had succeeded in doing, it is doubtful whether they
produced any more equitable or satisfactory results.

For nearly a year the jurisdiction of Governor
Harrison was extended over a vast area by an act of
Congress of March 26, 1804.[126] By this act the
District of Louisiana, comprising the country west
of the Mississippi and north of the thirty-third par-
allel, was attached to the Indiana Territory for administrative purposes. Under this arrangement a
number of laws were enacted, and an effort was made
to administer affairs in the new District. But the
inhabitants of the land west of the Mississippi were
opposed to this ''foreign'' government on general
principles and they protested vigorously against it.
The result was that on March 3, 1805, Congress
passed an act establishing the Territory of Louisiana
with its own government and officers.[127] The Governor and Judges of the Indiana Territory were later
given three hundred dollars each as ''compensation
for the extra services''.[128]

On the question of slavery, which was one of the
most prominent issues throughout the history of the
Indiana Territory, the people were divided. The
Ordinance of 1787 had prohibited slavery in the Old

Northwest, but during the early years of the Territorial government in Indiana a majority of the inhabitants were very much dissatisfied with this restriction, as was shown by frequent memorials and petitions.[129]   Governor Harrison personally seems to have favored the suspension of the prohibiting clause.[130]   At a convention held at Vincennes in December, 1802, over which Harrison presided, a memorial was sent to Congress favoring the suspension for a term of years of the sixth article of the Ordinance which prohibited slavery.[131] This proposition was rejected, however, since as a matter of fact Congress uniformly refused such petitions on the ground that they were contrary to the Ordinance. Later immigration so changed the sentiment of the Territory that it became very strongly anti-slavery.[132]

In 1805 Governor Harrison became convinced that the people desired an advance to the second stage of Territorial government, and accordingly he took the necessary steps to call an election of Representatives to a general assembly.   It is rather curious that a legislature was not demanded at an earlier day, but the explanation is doubtless to be found in Harrison's conciliatory policy.   In fact there seems to have been a desire on the part of a number of the people to proceed at once to the second stage after the organization of the Territory in 1800.   But a judicious letter by the Governor, in which he called attention to the increased burdens which such a step would entail, had a deterrent effect, and there was very little further agitation of the question for a number of years. Certain political considerations seem to have influenced the Governor as well as the people in 1805 when the government of the second stage was inaugurated.[133]

Another interesting illustration of the power of the Territorial Governor occurred in the year 1805. The newly elected House of Representatives had chosen the names of ten residents of the Territory from whom the President of the United States was to select five to form the Legislative Council. But President Jefferson waived his right of designation on the ground that "as the characters were unknown to him, it would be substituting chance for choice, were he to name the five councillors." Accordingly Governor Harrison was authorized to make the selection and return the names to the President for formal appointment, rejecting, however, "land-jobbers, dishonest men, and those who, though honest, might suffer themselves to be warped by party prejudices."[134] If the facts concerning the appointments had been known they doubtless would have caused ill-feeling toward Harrison on the part of the disappointed candidates, and so the public was kept in ignorance of the Governor's part in the choice until long afterwards.[135] The incident is an illustration of the manner in which the National government relied upon the soundness of the Governor's judgment.

The remainder of the civil history of the Indiana Territory is the story of a struggle for an enlargement of the rights of franchise, and of political contests in which Harrison took an active interest. The pacification of the Indians, the rapid settlement and cultivation of the country, and the special advantages enjoyed by the government from the first made the advancement of the Territory unusually rapid and gave an added stimulus to the desire for enlarged political opportunities. By memorials to Congress and by legislative enactments the people strove to extend the right of suffrage. Gradually the property qualification of voters was reduced until finally it was abolished entirely.[136] Likewise the people secured the right of electing the Territorial Delegate to Congress, as also the privilege of choosing the members of the Legislative Council — thus doing away with appointment by the President of the United States.[137]

In this way the people of the Indiana Territory procured a greater measure of democratic government than had been enjoyed in the Northwest Territory, or in fact than fell to the lot of some of the Territories later formed under the Ordinance. As has been seen, Indiana, while still a part of the Northwest Territory, had been well schooled in the preliminary steps of government, and so after a comparatively short time was better fitted to undertake some of the duties of self-government than the experience of most Territories would warrant at so

early a period in their development.   Indiana was
thus in some ways a rather precocious child of the
Territorial system and did not, perhaps, stand so
much in need of the fostering care and guidance of
a paternal hand.

The War of 1812 plunged the country into a
conflict for which there was not adequate preparation; and since the northern border was the fighting
line, the people of the exposed western frontier were
compelled to bear the brunt of numerous marauding
expeditions.   It is not within the province of these
pages to consider the campaigns of William Henry
Harrison or to describe the part played by the people
of the Indiana Territory in the War of 1812.[138]   In
fact, during that war, Harrison was the representative of the entire country and was fighting the
battles of the Nation.   His duties as General trans-
cended those of the governorship, and although he
took steps to protect his own Territory his activities
during this period were of a far broader significance.

Military duties now so engrossed the attention
of General Harrison that in February, 1813, President Madison nominated Thomas Posey for Governor of the Territory.[139]   For two years while
Harrison had, indeed, been almost constantly in the
field the gubernatorial functions had been exercised
by Secretary Gibson. Relieved of the routine work of
the civil office by the appointment of Posey, General
Harrison, now in charge of the Northwestern Army,

was enabled to concentrate his energy upon the vigorous prosecution of the war.

The character of the Indiana Territory was fully formed by this time, and the distinctive features of its growth and development were fixed — the personality of Governor Harrison having been stamped upon the institutions of the Territory. The few years of Territorial existence that remained under Governor Posey were mainly occupied in preparing for the State government that was soon to be established. The real work of the Territorial period had been done by Governor Harrison.

Indiana had grown rapidly in population. With 4,875 inhabitants in 1800, it had increased to 24,520 in 1810; and with the subsiding of hostilities and the lessening of danger on the frontier in 1814 the tide of immigration rose rapidly until in 1816 the population was 63,897.[140] The strides the Territory was making in population and in general development gave it strong claims for statehood; and on April 19, 1816, Congress passed an act enabling the inhabitants to form a constitution and organize a State government.[141] Pursuant thereto delegates were elected to a constitutional convention which met at Corydon (then the Territorial capital) June 10 to 29, 1816,[142] and drew up a constitution which was duly approved by Congress on December 11, 1816.[143] Thus Indiana became one of the States of the American Union.

Governor Harrison's administration may have

been less strenuous than St. Clair's from a strictly governmental standpoint, but it was more efficient. Harrison made himself a part of the Territory, fought its battles and administered its government — always keeping in mind the safety and interest of the people as a whole. He was too much of a soldier to forget that his real strength lay in the man who carried a gun, and too much of a politician to overlook the power of a vote. William Henry Harrison was a good leader, and his influence gave saneness and self-reliance to the institutional development of the Indiana Territory.

VII

GOVERNOR EDWARDS AND THE ILLINOIS
TERRITORY

When Congress in 1805 detached all that part of
the Indiana Territory north and east of the southern
extreme of Lake Michigan and called it the Territory of Michigan [144] there still remained a vast area
spreading from the Ohio State line to the Mississippi
River and extending northward to the Canadian
border. Much of this region was wild and uninhab-
ited, peopled only by traders and trappers or roving
Indians.

The main settlements were near Vincennes,
along the Ohio and Wabash rivers, and in the vicinity
of Kaskaskia.[145] These western settlements had
been established principally by the French coming
down from the north, and the people still found one
of their most natural avenues of supply through the
lakes and rivers to the northward. Physiographic
conditions tended to create a community of interest
among the people of the Illinois country which gradually developed into a sort of independence. Moreover, on account of their isolation they were politically somewhat neglected. Courts met but seldom,
and the local officers were widely scattered and felt
only an indifferent responsibility.

Isolation and the difficulties of administration, together with the desire for definite political privileges, soon prompted an agitation for a division into a separate Territory. Memorials were sent to Congress,[146] and the arguments upon the question became increasingly animated until the matter was taken up by the legislature of the Indiana Territory where the contention became more and more intense. Many of the people of Indiana opposed the division because it would increase the local taxation, while others objected because of the change in the center of influence that would result from the change in boundaries. Even in the Illinois country there was an anti-separationist faction.

The storm broke in 1808 at the time of the election of a Delegate to Congress. The Illinois members of the Territorial legislature of Indiana procured from one of the candidates a promise, guaranteed by his bond, to secure a division of the Territory if elected. Then in some way enough pledges were secured so that with the aid of the candidate's own vote he was elected.[147] Excitement ran high, the successful candidate was hung in effigy, and one of the partisans was shot and killed in an argument — so bitter did the feeling become.[148] The Delegate, however, secured the establishment of the Illinois Territory and discharged his bond, but "as it was doubtless desirable to change his residence, he came home with the commission for a federal judgeship

of the new territory in his pocket and removed to
Illinois."[149]

The Illinois Territory was set off by Congress
in an act of February 3, 1809, the provisions of which
were very similar to those of the act forming the
Indiana Territory. It provided for the exercise of
the same powers and duties by the Territorial officers, and guaranteed the inhabitants all the rights
and privileges granted by the Ordinance of 1787.
Profiting, however, by experience with the difficulties
which had arisen from the first division of the Northwest Territory, the framers of this act included express provisions for the disposition of pending suits
and for the collection of taxes due, the same as if the
Indiana Territory had remained undivided.[150]

The new Illinois Territory comprised all the
region from the Wabash River to the Mississippi,
extending northward from the Ohio River to the
Canadian border. It was an isolated strip of the
frontier, with Kaskaskia as its capital, and with
practically all of its settlements in the southern part.

In June, 1809, upon the recommendation of
Henry Clay,[151] President Madison appointed Ninian
Edwards, Chief Justice of Kentucky, as Governor of
the Illinois Territory. Governor Edwards was born
in Montgomery County, Maryland, in 1775, of
wealthy and well educated parents. He was given
a preparatory education, and at the age of nineteen
he entered college; but, becoming imbued with the
western fever, he went to Kentucky the following

year and began the study of law.[152]   "Distinguished
at that early age by his natural gifts and education,
as well as by his popular manners," says Mr. Washburne, editor of the *Edwards Papers,* "in less than
one year, and before he became of age, he was elected
to the Legislature of Kentucky from Nelson Co.;
and so satisfactorily did he discharge the duties of
that position, that he was reëlected to the same office
the subsequent year.   This was before he was admitted to the bar and while yet a student at law."[153]
In 1798 he received his license to practice law,[154] and
from that time on his promotion was rapid.   He
soon acquired a large practice, and was made Judge
of the Superior Court, and then Chief Justice of the
Court of Appeals of Kentucky.

A writer who knew Governor Edwards said of
him that "He was a bold, rather than a prudent,
politician — unwavering and untiring in the pursuit
of his object. From an intimate, acquaintance I can
say, that in the main, his views were honest, and that
he desired the best interests of the people.   His
personal appearance (for he was a gentleman of the
old school) was remarkably prepossessing, his manners polished, and his address attractive.   In private
life he was an enterprising citizen, an honest man,
and kind and attentive to the poor and deserv-
ing."[155]

The new Governor was in fact well fitted for the
position.   Although he lacked St. Clair's experience
in governmental affairs and Harrison's military

training, yet as a lawyer and judge he had acquired
a power of analyzing and dealing with complicated
problems which stood him in good stead as the chief
executive of a new country. Dignified in appearance and courteous in manner, sincere and unaffect-
ed, he seems to have won almost universal respect.
He was a persevering worker and was exact in the
discharge of every duty. Besides being Governor,
he was ex-officio Superintendent of Indian Affairs
and Superintendent of the United States Saline.
He was also largely interested in land speculation
and in extensive commercial transactions. In regard
to these latter activities, it is said that ''He established saw and grist mills, and stores in Kaskaskia,
Belleville, Carlisle, Alton, and Springfield in Illinois,
and at St. Louis, Chariton, and Franklin in Missouri;
he gave them his personal attention so far as was
consistent with his official duties, himself purchasing
the immense stocks of goods required.'' [156]

He seemed at times, when affairs of importance
pressed upon him, inclined to unnecessary solicitude
and anxiety,[157] which may perhaps be attributable to
the perturbed character of the times and to the difficult position in which he was placed. But the constant reiteration of his fears for the safety of the
Territory, though doubtless justified by actual conditions, leaves the impression of uneasiness of mind.
This does not mean, however, that Governor Edwards was of a vacillating temperament or lacked
the courage of his convictions, for the reverse is true.

He was, indeed, energetic and decisive above all things, and as the events of his administration show, resolutely carried out the policies upon which he had determined. He did not exhibit the scrupulous conscientiousness of St. Clair, nor even as fine a sense of duty as Governor Harrison,[158] but he was honest and fearless in the performance of what he considered his duty.

Nathaniel Pope was appointed Secretary of the Illinois Territory on March 7, 1809,[159] and on April 28 (Governor Edwards not having arrived) by proclamation he divided the Territory into two counties, St. Clair and Randolph, "for the prevention of crimes and injuries and for the execution of process civil and criminal within the Territory".[160] As Acting Governor, Pope from time to time issued commissions to justices of the peace, and to temporary military and county officers; but all of these appointments were to be valid only "during the pleasure of the Governor for the time being."[161] It was not until June 11, 1809, that Governor Edwards took the oath of office before Thomas Todd, Associate Justice of the Supreme Court, and began his administration of the Territory.[162]

Governor Edwards had scarcely set foot in the Territory before he was confronted with a situation which called for the utmost tact. The bitter animosities kindled by the fight for a division from Indiana still burned in the minds of the people, and the prospect of appointments under the new Governor

fanned the flames.   Upon his arrival at Kaskaskia
the Governor was welcomed by a deputation of citizens of Randolph County in an address of felicita-
tion.

But even on this occasion partisan motives appeared, for in the course of the address the delegates
stated that they hoped the Governor would "take
into consideration that the majority, whose incessant
exertions effectuated a division of the Territory,
have a claim on your excellency for the calumnies,
indignities and other enormities which those who opposed that measure never ceased to heap upon the
friends and advocates of the present system of our
government.   In announcing these truths . . . we
derive great consolation from a firm belief that your
excellency will gratify the virtuous majority, to
whose patriotic exertions the citizens are indebted
for a government of their choice, and your excellency
your high station, with that honorable indemnity
which is in your gift, and which would be considered
by them as a remuneration for all those indignities
and a pledge of their future support to your administration."

The Governor, however, was too discreet to be
drawn into the quarrel, and his reply was as fearless
as it was impartial.   "An office is a trust", he said,
"deposited in the hands of the individual, who holds
it not for his individual benefit and advantage, but
for the public good; and in all appointments by me
the public interest, and not a system of favoritism,

shall be my governing principle. A partisan I can not and will not be.''[163]

One faction urged him not to appoint as militia officers any persons who had ever opposed the division of the Territory, while another class proposed that all of the old officers be re-appointed. Some advised changes in some of the offices, while retaining the occupants of others. As the Governor was a stranger to these citizens and was as yet wholly dependent upon their information, he became greatly embarrassed ''by representations diametrically opposite to each other proceeding from sources apparently equally respectable.''[164]

This was indeed a dilemma; for in the state of public excitement any appointments that he might make would provoke hostility. But Governor Edwards was equal to the emergency. ''Revolving all these considerations and reflections in my own mind,'' he said, ''I determined, without such a suggestion from any person on earth, to adopt my own plan, which was that the companies should elect the company officers and that those should elect the field officers. . . . By my plan those officers who were meritorious would be most likely to succeed; those who were not so could have no cause for complaint. . . . I am not afraid to consult the people; and I do believe if in any case of militia appointments it is proper to consider their wishes it is in an exposed Territory like this, where the danger of invasion renders confidence in and attachment to officers so

indispensable to the service.''[165] Even such a fair
proposal as this was assailed on all sides and attacks
were made upon the Governor's motives. Edwards,
however, remained firm, ''determined to risk the
whole combined opposition of both parties rather
than yield myself up to the control or enlist under
the banners of either.''[166]

Such a course was almost unprecedented, and at
the time its wisdom was questioned in some quar-
ters;[167] but the National government had the good
sense to see the necessity for such a policy of con-
ciliation and the plan was approved.[168] The people
also, in time, began to appreciate the reasonableness
of the Governor's proposition; and after the election
of officers the differences disappeared to a great extent. Indeed, it was not long before a number of the
people asked for the privilege of electing their
county officers in the same way.[169]

There was a very urgent need of united action
on the part of the Governor and the people, since the
Illinois Territory was on the extreme frontier, surrounded by rivers and lakes, and therefore was easy
to attack but difficult to defend. The people were
poor, scattered, and ill prepared to protect themselves. The Indians were numerous and unremitting
in their depredations or secret hostility. Furthermore, the English in Canada were inclined to encourage dissatisfaction among the Red Men and to
nurture their resentment against the Americans.

As soon as Governor Edwards had established
the civil government of the Territory he turned his
attention to the needs arising from its exposed condition.   The restlessness of the Indians and the frequent reports of their depredations impressed him
with the necessity of investigating the situation
thoroughly.   He employed several loyal French
traders and interpreters who were well acquainted
with the Indians and who went out among the tribes
and reported actual conditions to the Governor.

Edwards also had several councils with the Indians, and held frequent interviews with their chiefs.
The Indians appeared friendly and gave assurances
that the depredations would cease and that they
would dwell in peace with their American brothers.
But the Governor was not misled.   As a result of
the information which he secured, he soon became
convinced that the Illinois Indians were organizing
and preparing to open hostilities upon the white
settlements when an opportune time should arrive.
The voluminous correspondence of Governor Edwards and his many letters during this period fur-
nish ample proof that he realized the danger and
repeatedly urged the necessity of protective measures.[171]

A militia company had been organized in St.
Clair County before the Governor's arrival; and
from time to time companies were formed in the
various settlements.   But detached companies could
not cover the vast region of the Territory, and they

were practically powerless when it came to protecting the isolated and widely scattered frontier settlements which were in fact the most in need of help. These conditions justified the anxiety of Governor Edwards, and, urged on by the repeated appeals of the people, he continued his efforts to secure assistance.[172]

During the year 1810 the Indians continued restless and several cases of murder were reported.[173] In the spring and summer of 1811 depredations were so frequent and murders so numerous that the people became very much alarmed.   A mass meeting of the citizens of St. Clair County, in October, 1811, drew up a memorial to the Governor, calling attention to the grave dangers that menaced the Territory, expressing confidence in the Governor, and exhorting him, as the constitutional channel between the people and the general government, to secure more garrisons and more military supplies for the better protection of the frontier.   A memorial to be forwarded to the President of the United States was also enclosed.[174]

The Territory itself, under the direction of Governor Edwards, raised four companies of mounted rangers and began active preparations for defense.[175] Block-houses surrounded by strong stockades were erected in a number of the settlements, and at other places larger forts were built.   The block-houses were built of logs, one story and a half high and with heavily barred doors.   They were well supplied with port-holes; and the upper story projected somewhat over the first, thus allowing ample means for watching the movements of the enemy. The stockades were made large enough to accommodate the settlers of the vicinity and their property. Cabins were usually built within the enclosure and a well was dug to supply water in case of siege. The forts were larger, being a series of block-houses connected by stockades.[176] These frontier posts very effectively protected the settlers who with their stock and other belongings sought shelter therein. Nearly all of the later tragedies were enacted at isolated settlements, or where scattered settlers braved the dangers alone or incautiously traveled from place to place.

The dispatches and reports which came to the Governor indicated that ''The Prophet'', a talented Shawnee leader, was carefully planning to strike the Illinois settlements, preparatory to an attack on Vincennes and other important settlements, and that the coöperation of various other tribes was expected.[177] Governor Edwards, seeing that the Peoria Lake region was the seat of most of the trouble, determined to send an expedition to that point for the purpose of over-aweing the Indians and also for the capture if possible of some of the fugitive Indian murderers and the recovery of some of the stolen property. He accordingly commissioned Captain Samuel Levering, who with a few men set out on July 25, 1811.

Upon arrival at their destination Levering and his men were received by Gomo, the Pottawattamie

Chief, who gave them assurances that the murderers would be given up and that he would do all in his power to restore the stolen property. At one of the many conferences and councils which were held with the Indians a speech of Governor Edwards was read, and Gomo and Little Chief each responded. They were profuse in their promises; but when the council adjourned the Captain returned without any prisoners, and it was later learned that some of the murderers were sitting in the very council.[178] The guilty Indians, having thus escaped punishment, became more bold and troublesome than before.

It was this feature of Indian diplomacy that troubled Governor Edwards more than any other problem connected with the Indian affairs. A firm and just administration of the laws was absolutely essential in dealing with the Indians. Yet when a murder was committed or property was stolen it was next to impossible to identify the culprits owing to the confusing Indian names, the constant roving of the various bands of Red Men, and the savage cunning with which the deed was always committed. The difficulty was increased by the fact that the Chiefs were usually either distinctly hostile to the Americans or rendered passive by the fear of antagonizing their own people. Moreover, since the Indians were rarely brought to account it became increasingly difficult to restrain the soldiers and settlers who took matters in their own hands — sometimes wreaking vengeance upon the innocent in their

fury at the barbarous practices of the Red Men.[179]
Meantime the Indian barbarities became more and
more frequent and were a constant menace to the
safety of the people of the country.

Evidence was also accumulating in abundance
which proved that the English were doing all in their
power to encourage hostility towards the Americans;
while by extensive gifts of supplies and trinkets, and
by friendly overtures they sought to attach the Indians strongly to themselves.[180]   Indeed, the committee appointed by the House of Representatives
to investigate the conditions on the frontier reported
on June 13, 1812, that there was no doubt but that
the British were furnishing supplies to the Indians,
and that the Indians were making such hostile
preparations that it was necessary to proceed at
once to protect the frontiers from the attack with
which they were threatened.[181]

It was expected that General Harrison's victory
at Tippecanoe would have a deterrent effect upon
the Indians, but it was in reality offset by the influence of the British and the activities of the Shawnee
Prophet.   War with Great Britain now seemed inevitable.   Malden on the Canadian border was the
distributing point from which Indian supplies were
given out and from which the British influence emanated; and the country of the Old Northwest became
the field for a desperate border warfare.

The beginning of the year 1812 found both sides
making preparations for the struggle.   The Indians,

urged on by the British and aroused by the eloquence of the Shawnee Prophet and his brother Tecumseh, were forming an extensive confederation of the tribes to coöperate against the Americans. The Americans, on the other hand, were doing what they could to keep the tribes friendly and to prevent further Indian barbarities. In April, 1812, Governor Edwards made another effort to conciliate the Indians by inviting a number of the most influential chiefs of the Pottawattamies, Kickapoos, Ottawas, and Chippewas to meet him in council at Cahokia. At the council the Governor delivered a long "talk", and Gomo made reply in behalf of the assembled chiefs. He complained of some things the Americans had done, but said the punishment the Indians had received at Tippecanoe had frightened them; and he promised that his people would never join the British or break their peace with the Americans.[182]

This council, like the others, accomplished nothing; and the Indians after having been well fed and royally entertained returned to their warlike preparations very well satisfied with themselves. Governor Edwards, moreover, was well aware that the Indians were carrying on a deceptive game, for in writing to Governor Harrison about the council he declared that there was but "little dependence to be placed on their professions", and in his report to the National government he expressed the same opinion even more forcibly.[183] Consequently he continued to urge more effective means of protection;

and while waiting for Congress to act he busied himself with endeavors to strengthen the frontier forces and to mitigate the horrors of Indian barbarities.

The National government was beginning to realize, what Governor Edwards and General Harrison had so long urged, that the frontier was poorly guarded. In fact the War Department had really done very little for frontier protection in the Territories. The Adjutant General's report of June 6, 1812, showed that the following number of regular soldiers were stationed in or on the borders of the Illinois Territory: at Fort Massac, 35; at Fort Madison, 44; at Fort Dearborn, 53; and at Vincennes and in the vicinity, 117; while the arms and munitions were hardly more than were needed in time of peace.[184]

Indeed, the Territory would have fared very badly if it had not been for the Territorial militia, which at this time numbered about four regiments and consisted mostly of mounted rangers. From all reports these rangers were aggressive and tireless in their efforts to protect the settlements, and by their efficient service materially lessened the number of Indian outrages.

On June 18, 1812, war was formally declared with Great Britain.[185] But it was not until August that the first severe blows fell, when the terrible massacre at Fort Dearborn [186] gave the Indians renewed courage, and the disgraceful capitulation of Hull at Detroit imperiled the northern border.

It is needless in this connection to recite the well known events of the war. The campaigns of 1812 and 1813 were disastrous. In 1814, the bloodiest year of the war, the Americans gained but little advantage. During all this time the people of the western Territories were practically left to protect themselves as best they could against British marauding parties and Indian raids. Governor Edwards on several occasions during the war found it necessary to remonstrate against the concentration of troops in Indiana, where they were not so much needed, because the population was larger and hence able to put a larger force of volunteers in the field, and because troops from the eastern States could be brought into Indiana on shorter notice.[187]

Another difficulty lay in the fact that it was impossible to get troops from Kentucky. Governor Edwards had been authorized by the Secretary of War to call upon the Governor of Kentucky for assistance; and Governor Scott and later Governor Shelby of Kentucky had promised troops. Yet on one occasion Edwards publicly stated that "Not a man has arrived" and even Colonel Russell's force had been called off to Vincennes, "leaving us to shift for ourselves, without the aid of a single man who has not been raised in the Territory." [188]

At times Edwards also took issue with General Harrison on the plan of campaign. In the fall of 1812, when it was Harrison's plan to prosecute a campaign to aid Hull, Governor Edwards vigorously opposed it on the ground that it would leave the frontier exposed.[189]   Throughout the war the Governor devoted himself almost entirely to measures for the safety of his Territory — the one aim that seemed uppermost in his mind.   And whenever he became convinced that pacific means were of no avail, he personally conducted expeditions against the Indian villages to stamp out the cause of the frontier troubles.[190]

The chief events in the Illinois country preceding the declaration of war in 1812 have been considered at some length as showing the trend of Illinois Territorial history during this period.   Nor is it necessary to continue this phase of the subject further, since the events already described are characteristic of the whole period.

These were indeed turbulent times on the Illinois frontier.   There could be little civil development in the Territory when the whole attention of the administration was concentrated upon the effort to effectually protect the inhabitants.   Immigration was at a standstill during the war, and the continual danger had a deterrent effect upon all forms of improvement.

The feeling of insecurity was increased by the fact that the land office officials were slow in making adjustments.   Many bitter enemies were made by their wholesale rejection of claims and their indiscriminate accusations of forgery and perjury.[191] The settlers dared not make improvements; and in

the general insecurity of titles few bought land and
few extensive settlements were made.   Governor Edwards at various times urged the passage of laws
giving the right of preëmption to actual settlers and
affording the settlers better opportunities at the land
sales.[192]   In 1813 the right of preëmption was granted,[193] thus removing one of the greatest barriers to
the development of the western country.

In the midst of the ravages of war the civil administration of the Territory was carried on as uniformly as possible.   When the Territory was first
separated from Indiana, the Governor and Judges
had met and reënacted the Indiana laws, and these
stood with few changes until the election of a legislature.[194]

Illinois naturally inherited the county system
of local government, which through southern and
middle State influences had prevailed in the Northwest Territory and in Indiana.   In fact most of the
people in southern Illinois during Territorial days
were from the South or had come under southern influence.[195]   Indiana had definitely established
counties by law in 1807,[196] and this law was reënacted
by the Illinois Territorial legislature in 1812,[197] thus
giving legal sanction to a system that had been tacit-
ly followed since the organization of the Territory.
This system of local government remained unchanged until the preponderance of New Englanders
succeeded, some time after the formation of the State

government, in forcing a recognition of the town meeting.[198]

Under the law creating the Illinois Territory the Governor was empowered to call an election for members of a legislature at any time when he became convinced that a majority of the freeholders desired it.[199] The peculiar conditions existing in the Territory, however, caused Governor Edwards to hesitate before calling such an election. Owing to the land difficulties and the delay in the sales few settlers had titles to their lands. They were ''squatters'' and had in fact settled illegally upon the land, no matter how good citizens they were or whether they had made improvements in good faith or not. On several occasions the Governor pointed out the fact that of the respectable and bona fide farmers who settled in the Territory not more than one-tenth were freeholders.[200] This would put into the hands of a very small minority the power to decide whether or not there should be a change to the second stage of government and to dictate the selection of the members of the assembly. Thus the property qualification became a serious restriction of the right of suffrage.

Moreover, Governor Edwards stated that he did not know of a single person qualified to act as Representative by possessing the necessary freehold of two hundred acres of land required by the Ordinance, nor were there in his opinion more than three or four who had a freehold of fifty acres qualifying them to vote.[201] Although he hesitated for these reasons to call an election, Edwards nevertheless felt the necessity of having a Delegate in Congress to plead the cause of the Territory and look after its interests. In St. Clair's time the recommendations of the Governor had usually been sufficient, but now with the increasing business of Congress and the distracting events of a great war more direct influence was necessary. This need for a Territorial Delegate illustrates the growth of a new idea. The Delegate had always been an important factor, but now the Governor had come to look upon him as necessary in order to obtain a just measure of rights for the Territory. Consequently, Edwards advocated the extension of suffrage to all citizens, regardless of property qualifications, and the election of the Delegate directly by the people instead of by the legislature.[202]

Soon afterwards Congress passed an act extending the right of suffrage to all white male persons twenty-one years of age, who had paid a Territorial tax and lived one year within the Territory. Furthermore, the people were given the right to vote not only for Representatives, but also for members of the Legislative Council and Delegate to Congress.[203] Thus at one stroke many obstacles to Territorial development were removed, and the people of the Illinois Territory gained the same privileges as had previously been extended to the inhabitants of Indiana. Governor Edwards was largely instrumental

in securing these rights for the people, even though
his own power was curtailed to a certain extent
thereby, and the incident is an example of his self-
sacrificing loyalty to the Territory.

Edwards had for some time been convinced that
the people desired the change to the second grade of
government, and now that the objections to such a
change had been overcome, he decided to submit the
question to a vote of the people. The result showed
that public sentiment was overwhelmingly in favor
of entering upon the second stage,[204] and consequently an election was called at which a Delegate to Congress and members of the legislature were duly
elected.

On November 25, 1812, the new legislature convened at Kaskaskia and proceeded at once to business.[205] In the first place they reënacted such laws
of Indiana as had not been repealed by Governor Edwards and the Judges of the Illinois Territory at an
earlier date. Then followed laws of every description. In the criminal code there were continued the
harsh measures of the Indiana Territory — and if
anything, punishments were made even more severe.
Branding a letter ''T'' with a red hot iron upon the
hand was the penalty for a second conviction of having altered or defaced the brands on domestic ani-
mals. Confinement in the stocks and the pillory,
fines and imprisonment, and whipping on the naked
back from ten to five hundred lashes according to the
offence, were among the penalties provided.[206]

An attempt on the part of the legislature in 1814 to reorganize the judiciary in such a manner as to materially modify the provisions of the Ordinance gave rise to a friendly controversy between the Governor and the Judges. The power of the legislature to pass such a law was questioned. At the request of the assembly the Judges prepared an opinion stating emphatically that "the court established by the ordinance cannot be subject to the revision or control of any tribunal established by the Territorial Legislature".[207] The views of the Governor were also requested, and he prepared an answer in which he contended that the legislature had full power to provide for the affairs of the Territory and to establish a general judicial system.[208] Being still in doubt, however, the legislature decided to leave the matter to Congress with a petition that the law be declared legal "in order to remove any future or existing difficulties that may arise between the Judges and the Legislature."[209] Such action was accordingly taken by Congress;[210] and it is to be presumed that both of the contending parties believed that the validity of their arguments was amply vindicated. This small controversy indicates the cordial relations which existed between Governor Edwards and the other branches of the Territorial government.

The greatest difficulty which the Governor had to face was the slowness and indifference of the National government. Time and again his plans for the Territory were thwarted by the inaction of

officials in the East who could seldom appreciate the
real situation in the West.   His letters and papers
are full of appeals for help to meet the pressing
needs of the Territory; and although his persistence
was often rewarded in the end, many wise plans were
defeated by the delay and neglect of those in authority.[211]   The war and the consequent necessity of a
system of military discipline tended toward requirements of stricter accountability and a more uniform
reliance on orders direct from headquarters.   St.
Clair and Harrison had been given a much freer rein
at first, but the web of officialism and red-tape had
now begun to spread out and around the Territorial
Governor.

Besides the duties of the governorship, Edwards
performed various other functions which deserve
some mention.   As Superintendent of Indian Affairs his activities did not vary greatly from those
of St. Clair or Harrison.   The records show that
Governor Edwards negotiated nineteen Indian treaties during his administration,[212] and other incidents
in his dealings with the Indians have already been
related.   He was also Superintendent of the United
States Saline; the general government having retained control of the salt works in Illinois.   The
Governor's duties as Superintendent consisted of
making contracts for leasing the salt works, collect-
ing the rent in salt, and providing for the shipment
and sale of the government's share.   That these
duties were burdensome as well as important is

shown in the number of letters on this subject in the correspondence of Governor Edwards.[213]

After the close of the war the tide of immigration flowed steadily into Illinois. At first the settlers were mostly from the South, and during the greater part of the Territorial period Illinois was largely influenced by southerners. But towards the last years of the period the northern element began to increase until it changed the complexion of the Territory, showing itself not only in changes in local government, but also in finally making Illinois a free instead of a slave State.

In its institutional development the Illinois Territory presents few novel features. Its history is very largely the story of further progress along lines already begun in the Northwest Territory and the Indiana Territory. Indeed, these Territories present a consistent and continuous course of government along related lines. Governor Edwards, like his predecessors, was the dominating influence. He had won the confidence of the people during the first years of his administration and he was naturally continued in office until the admission of Illinois as a State in 1818.

Governor Edwards loved Illinois, and every act of his was influenced by his desire to build up the Territory. For him the office of Governor meant an opportunity to labor and plan for the general welfare. The prerogatives of his office were but means to an end. His sincerity and industry were unquestioned; while his firmness and his conciliatory policy, together with his deserved popularity, resulted in harmony among the various elements in the Territory.   Ninian Edwards had become so closely identified with the Illinois country that when the State was admitted in 1818 [214] and his work as Territorial Governor was ended, he settled down to a life of larger service for the Commonwealth.

GOVERNOR HULL AND THE TERRITORY OF MICHIGAN

With the formation of the Territory of Michigan in 1805 a new line of western development was opened. For nearly two centuries the extreme Northwest had been tributary to Canada and subject to its influence. French traders and trappers had roamed over the country, devout priests had endeavored repeatedly to christianize the aboriginal tribes, and some attempts had been made at settlement. After Wolfe's victory on the Plains of Abraham, the English also exerted an influence over this region from the north, until the Old Northwest was wrested from them by the conquest of George Rogers Clark.

The change in political allegiance, however, did not alter the social and racial conditions on the northern border. The hauling down of a flag may determine the question of sovereignty; but the social life of the people, their inherent political ideas and customs, their racial tendencies, and the general conditions by which they are environed are not so easily eradicated or overcome. Ohio, Indiana, and Illinois, being in the natural line of the westward movement, had been settled rapidly by Americans and had developed characteristic Anglo-Saxon institutions

which soon led to statehood. But Michigan, cut off
by the lakes and other physiographic barriers, had
been influenced from the valley of the St. Lawrence,
and consequently was very different in spirit and
development from the country along the Ohio.

Such was the condition of Michigan when it began its Territorial existence in 1805. Isolated geo-
graphically and alien by natural tendency, it had a
long and trying history before it became genuinely
American and ready for statehood.

The act of Congress which divided the Indiana
Territory provided that all that part "which lies
north of a line drawn east from the southerly bend
or extreme of Lake Michigan, until it shall intersect
Lake Erie, and east of a line drawn from the said
southerly bend through the middle of said lake to
its northern extremity, and thence due north to the
northern boundary of the United States" should
constitute the Territory of Michigan. It was enacted
that the government of the new Territory should be
in all respects similar to that provided by the Ordinance of 1787, and that the inhabitants should enjoy
all the rights and privileges guaranteed by that
Ordinance. The officers were to have the same powers, duties, and compensation as provided by the laws
of the United States for similar offices in the Indiana
Territory.[215] In fact the Organic Act of the Territory of Michigan was practically identical with the
acts establishing the Indiana and Illinois Territories.

President Jefferson appointed General William Hull of Massachusetts as the first Governor of the new Territory; and, although the General was an accomplished gentleman, a competent executive, and a man of extensive and favorable reputation, the choice was anything but fortunate.   As Mr. Cooley has said, "had he been made the executive of a staid and orderly commonwealth, with associates in government of similar characteristics, his administration might have been altogether popular and successful. But in Michigan he found uncongenial people all about him, and it soon appeared that he was somewhat lacking in the persistent self-assertion necessary to make the rough characters of a backwoods settlement recognize and accept the fact that within the proper limits of his authority he proposed to be and would be ruler and master." [216]

Unfortunately the Chief Justice, Augustus B. Woodward, was diametrically the opposite of the Governor, both in disposition and methods, and he was intolerant of opposition.   But in spite of the fact that he was somewhat eccentric, Woodward was an exceptionally able lawyer, and the brunt of the labor in framing the laws fell upon him.[217]   Indeed, the compiled laws of 1805 were popularly known as *Woodward's Code*.   This compilation embodied the results of the early efforts of the Governor and Judges to formulate laws for the Territory.   The Code of the Northwest Territory, having been handed down to Indiana and Illinois, became the basis of jurisprudence in those Territories, and alterations were made from time to time to keep pace with the changing conditions. But Michigan, being different in situation and having peculiar conditions to meet, struck out alone and enacted a new code of laws especially adapted to the situation of the new Territory.

In the sessions of the Governor and Judges as a law-making body there was great unanimity in the passage of the laws. The only disagreements were upon the old question as to what constituted ''a majority of the Governor and Judges'', and upon the necessity of enacting laws only of the original States.[218]

Since the first experiments of Governor St. Clair and the Judges of the Northwest Territory, Congress had looked with much disfavor upon the practice of enacting laws *de novo*; and so the strict letter of the Ordinance was now complied with. In *Woodward's Code* the original statute from which the law was taken was always indicated, being considered as much a part of the law as the title or enacting clause. This method of law-making was not accepted, however, without a protest, and Governor Hull in a report to the President argued strongly and at some length in favor of repealing this unnecessary, awkward, and non-republican restriction.[219] A local writer of that time declared that the Governor and Judges would ''parade the laws of the original States before them on the table, cull letters

from the laws of Maryland, syllables from the laws
of Virginia, words from the laws of New York, sentences from the laws of Pennsylvania, verses from
the laws of Kentucky, and chapters from the laws of
Connecticut.'' [220]   This contemporary burlesque, in
spite of its exaggeration, emphasized what the Governors had repeatedly stated — that there was no
logical or practical necessity for such a limitation
upon the law-making power.   No law in all its details will fit two different conditions; but by this
system the bad and unsuitable parts must be adopted
with the good.   It set a premium upon the promis-
cuous taking of general laws, instead of encouraging
a careful selection of the best from all sources to
meet special needs.   It would seem that the participation of the Governor in legislation and the super-
visory control of Congress were sufficient checks
without the addition of such a troublesome limitation.

Thanks to the energy of Judge Woodward the
code of 1805 was completed without delay — in spite
of the undercurrent of dissension in its preparation
— and was duly enacted as the law of the Territory.

When Governor Hull first came to the Territory
he found the once thriving town of Detroit, the capital of the Territory, wiped out completely by a dev-
astating fire, and the people homeless and in want.
Steps were at once taken to relieve the suffering.
A temporary town was laid out, and soon thereafter
courts were established to settle existing business.

The militia was also organized and brought into the field for the protection of property.   With these temporary expedients established, Congress was importuned to empower the Governor and Judges to make permanent enactments regarding the land.[221]

In the spring of 1806 Congress passed an act granting a tract of ten thousand acres of land upon and adjacent to the old site of Detroit, and the Governor and Judges were authorized to lay out a new town and give land to the American citizens made destitute by the fire.[222]   The Governor and Judges thus became a board of apportionment and equalization, and they were also empowered to sit as a court to hear and adjust claims arising as a consequence of such grants of land.   These sittings gave frequent opportunities for the incompatible tempers of the Governor and the Chief Justice to clash.

One writer says that "as one of the associate judges took sides with the governor and the other against him, the meetings of the four, whether as a land board or as a legislature, were occasions for undignified and angry contests and dissentions which were well calculated to bring public authority into contempt.   It does not appear that the governor was wanting in proper observance of the proprieties of his station, or of the rules of law; but his antagonist was less scrupulous, and by his very audacity not only for the most part carried his points, but also carried with him an apparent public sentiment. He [Woodward] was ingenious in finding ways to annoy and mortify the governor, and his own misbehavior furnished opportunities when nothing else did."[223]

The French and other foreigners, as well as the Canadians and Indians, had paid little attention to their titles, and the confusion and conflict of evidence, together with the obliteration of many landmarks by the fire, threw the whole question of land distribution into an interminable tangle.[224] These conditions and the consequent wrangles of the authorities resulted in an uncertain and vacillating policy, and nothing of consequence was accomplished until long after the fire. In the meantime all business in the Territory was at a standstill.[225]

Governor Hull also found that the duties of Superintendent of Indian Affairs were unexpectedly difficult and onerous. He discovered that the "plans made by a New England fireside for the amelioration of the aboriginal conditions" were sadly deficient when it came to practical application, and that his own æsthetic and pacific nature was unfitted to brave the wilds of the frontier on the dangerous mission of placating the savages.[226] The Indians were restless throughout the West, and the British influence from over the border enhanced their ill-feeling and resentment. Even the activity of General Harrison and his victory at Tippecanoe did not entirely curb the Indian barbarities in isolated regions. It was too much of a problem for Governor Hull, and although he negotiated a few treaties he was glad to leave the general control of Indian affairs in the hands of General Harrison.

Governor Hull's rather unfortunate administration culminated in the surrender of Detroit to the British at the very beginning of the War of 1812.[227] He gave up the town completely — prompted, it is said, by the humanitarian motive of protecting the citizens from Indian barbarities — without a stroke in its defense. Such an ignominious surrender aroused the resentment of the whole people; and when it was followed by an arbitrary and oppressive military government by the British the cup of bitterness was almost full.

The action of Chief Justice Woodward in remaining at his post and assisting the British in civil affairs after the surrender was much criticised. But in a vigorous letter to Secretary of State Monroe he stated that he did so for the purpose of protecting American interests and assisting his fellow citizens as much as possible, and that he did not receive any remuneration from the British nor did he perform any official act.[228] In spite of Woodward's efforts the interregnum of English military rule was nevertheless a heavy yoke upon the people; and although the American laws and courts were continued, the galling exercise of arbitrary power was eased but very little. The coming of the American army which released the inhabitants from this thralldom was hailed with joy.[229]

The history of the Michigan frontier during the war would form a volume in itself. In this connection it is sufficient to bear in mind that the ravages of war and the interrupted development of those uncertain times, combined with a constantly changing civil and military government, left Michigan in a somewhat chaotic condition.

With the government of the Territory hopelessly demoralized, and the danger, treachery and destitution prevailing along the border, the need of a vigorous executive became imperative. President Madison selected for the task a young man who was aggressive and fearless, schooled in the privations of a frontier soldier's life, but with a wide experience and a capacity for statecraft — Lewis Cass.[230]

GOVERNORS CASS AND MASON AND THE TERRITORY OF MICHIGAN

The task that confronted Governor Cass in 1813 was a stupendous one. The changing fortunes of the war had left the Territory in a state of disorganization. The civil system was razed to the ground: not one stone was left upon another. The troops had been withdrawn for the eastern campaigns, leaving only a handful of soldiers with inadequate equipment to defend the border. The Indians, made bold by the license of war and incited by English influence, murdered and plundered the people almost without restraint; and even the friendly tribes had become treacherous and uncertain.

With the whole country pillaged and devastated the people were in actual want, and starvation stared them in the face. The French settlers especially, with their usual resources exhausted, and unable in their easy-going way to provide for such an emergency, were in destitute circumstances. The poor settlers from the Raisin River, whose homes had been burned and whose crops and belongings had been destroyed, were in dire need of clothing and the necessities of life. Business and trade were everywhere practically suspended. The currency was de-

preciated and unstable. The government stores
were used to supply the most pressing needs, but
they were inadequate; and even the special appropriations secured from Congress scarcely more than
tided the people over some of the more deplorable
situations. The sinister clouds of want and despair
hung darkly over the Territory of Michigan.[231]

Throughout Governor Cass grappled with the
problems with energy and decision. He distributed
the public stores with discriminating judgment
where they were most needed to ward off actual
starvation; and he did all in his power to secure aid
and appropriations from the general government.
His first thought was for the starving and desolate
inhabitants, and he worked with tireless energy for
their relief during the whole period of the war when
the suffering was the greatest.

The Governor saw clearly that confidence must
be restored. Progress was impossible with the people huddled like frightened sheep around the forts
and villages, or barricaded within their own homes
and startled into feverish preparation for defense at
the slightest noise. Without delay a volunteer company was formed and Cass led them boldly against
the Indians. His dashing bravery was contagious
and so inspired his soldiers that they completely
routed the Indians in a fierce engagement. This victory the Governor followed up with a relentless perseverance which soon brought the tribes to terms.
Confidence thus restored acted like magic upon the

Territory. The people began to appreciate their fearless and practical Governor, and they rallied to his assistance.

But all through the period of the war Cass was greatly hampered by the lack of military authority and assistance. No military commission had been issued to him since his appointment as Governor, and as a civil officer he had little authority over the small garrison and very little control over the few troops who were continually being hurried off to eastern battlefields.

In the meantime the Governor was diligently restoring the local government of the Territory. The parts of the system which were the most essential were at once reorganized. Courts were established, local officers and magistrates appointed, and the Territory laid out into administrative divisions. Much care was exercised in the selection of officers — although difficulty was occasioned by the indifference of the French and Canadian elements in the population. But Cass was an enthusiastic, patriotic American, and he began the task of instilling American principles with characteristic vigor and thoroughness. Nothing was left undone to make the local governments as effective as possible.

As the population increased the Governor gave greater rein to his decided democratic views by allowing the people to express their wishes at every possible opportunity. It was his custom to send out blank commissions and permit the people to select

certain officers by local elections, although he thus
voluntarily curtailed his own right of appointment.[232]
He did not hesitate to put into practice his often repeated doctrine that the people were the true source
of power in government and that they should have
a direct voice in political affairs.

So eagerly did Governor Cass press on towards
self-government for the Territory that in 1818 he
called for a vote of the people on the question of
whether or not they desired to enter upon the second
stage of political organization under the Ordinance.
The people, however, not being ready for the change,
voted down the proposition; and it was not until
1823 that the second stage of government was adopted and a legislature elected.

The subject of land titles gave the officials in
Michigan considerable trouble, just as it had the
earlier Governors in the Old Northwest. Although
portions of the Michigan country had been settled
for over one hundred and fifty years, only eight regular titles were found.[233]   Exhaustive investigations
and reports were made upon the subject, and at last
a committee of the House of Representatives recommended a liberal land policy as the truest economy
and the surest means of binding the frontier people
to the government by ties of interest and friendship.[234]

A law was accordingly passed by Congress ap-
proving the report of the land commissioners at Detroit and confirming title in actual settlers within

the districts where Indian titles had been extinguished and where such title did not conflict with
United States registration and reservations.   The
same act gave the commissioners summary power to
decide upon land claims outside of Detroit.[235]   Subsequent acts were passed from time to time confirming and enlarging the rights of settlers and granting
them the right of preëmption.[236]   Governor Cass was
a firm believer in this policy, and continually urged
the sale of land in smaller subdivisions to actual
settlers.[237]

The Territory of Michigan was at the start discredited by the government surveyors who came to
run the meridian line for the purpose of surveying
the bounty and other government lands.   These surveyors, either unnerved by the hardships and difficulties of the task or indifferent to their duties, returned after a short time and reported that the interior of Michigan was a cheerless wilderness of
swamps and sand, very little of it being fit for cultivation.

Acting on this report, the President in his message of 1816 advised Congress to locate the bounty
lands for soldiers in more fertile portions of the
Northwest.[238]   This official condemnation spread
throughout the East and prospective settlers
shunned the Michigan country as they would an infected district.   It was difficult to overcome this
groundless prejudice, and Governor Cass worked for
years to restore the confidence of the government

and of the people in the fertile lands of Michigan. In furtherance of this object he led an extensive exploring expedition out through the western section of the Territory, taking with him scientists of ability, whose reports of the wonderful fertility of the region and of its vast undeveloped resources helped to allay the distrust and encourage immigration.[240]

Works of internal improvement were also begun, such as the building of public roads, which greatly facilitated immigration and communication between various sections of the Territory. Governor Cass labored tirelessly and effectively for the welfare of his Territory, and he was rewarded by a rapid increase in population and material prosperity.

The extinguishment of the Indian title to the land and the pacification of hostilely inclined Red Men was a much more difficult and delicate matter. It required great personal exertion as well as courage, tact, and resourcefulness. Governor Cass traveled over the Territory, riding hundreds of miles on horseback or in boats to the furthest districts, in order to negotiate treaties, quell uprisings, or strengthen the friendship of the Indians.

It has been estimated that there were over forty-one thousand Indians in the Territory of Michigan at this time;[241] and as Governor Cass was ex-officio Superintendent of Indian Affairs, his responsibilities were great. He took a broad view of the question and seems always to have had the interest and welfare of the Indians at heart. He continually encour-

aged industry and civilizing tendencies among them
— especially when dispensing government stores and
treaty payments — and he sought vigorously to prevent the use of "fire water". It is said that on one
occasion, to emphasize the fact that the government
was not actuated by parsimonious motives in this
matter, he knocked in the heads of several casks of
liquor and allowed the contents to run out on the
ground, amid the despairing protests of the thirsty
warriors.[242]   He always dealt fairly and honestly
with the Indians, kept his word at any cost, and endeavored at all times to have his treaty pledges and
payments punctually and fully carried out.

The Governor's knowledge of Indian character
was remarkable, and his actions at crucial moments
were courageous and firm. It is related that on one
of his expeditions his small company came upon a
large Indian encampment where the braves had
donned their war paint and were in an ugly mood.
The Governor endeavored to arrange a council, but
the Indians were openly hostile and impudent.
Finally the savages retired to their camp and delib-
erately hoisted a British flag. Governor Cass without a moment's hesitation, alone and unarmed, strode
into their midst, hauled down the flag and trampled
it under his feet, telling them in strong terms that
two flags could not float over the same land, and that
the Great American Father would certainly crush
them if they were not faithful. The Indians, dis-
mayed by this display of courage, gave up their war-

like intentions and signed the treaty which the Governor drew up for them.[243]   It was his courage and his thorough knowledge of Indian traits which made Cass so successful in his administration of Indian affairs.   In addition to all the other work he accomplished along this line, he negotiated eighteen Indian treaties during his administration.   Some of these treaties were very important and involved the cession to the United States of vast tracts of land, which were thus rendered accessible for settlement and improvement.[244]

The flag incident is illustrative of another difficulty which Governor Cass had to contend against to a greater degree even than the other Territorial Governors in the Old Northwest during this period — namely, the insidious British influence across the border.   As has already been stated, the English agents in Canada continued to distribute presents to the Indians and persistently sought to poison their minds against the Americans long after the war had ceased.   The desire to retain control of the fur trade, as well as a desire for revenge, perpetuated this policy.   The presence of the British flag in the Indian camp was strong evidence of British persuasion, and made plain the source of hostility and discontent. Two other instances will further illustrate this point.

Colonel James, the commander of a small British post across the border, notified Governor Cass that an Indian had been murdered by American soldiers and intimated that savage vengeance would be

the result if the culprit was not summarily punished.
Governor Cass replied that he would investigate the
case and that he felt confident that justice would provide punishment commensurate with the crime.
Later, having gone thoroughly into the facts, Cass
wrote to Colonel James that the Indian was killed
while attempting to shoot an American soldier, that
the affair had occurred within the Territorial jurisdiction of the United States, and that the laws of the
Territory provided for the punishment of the offender and afforded ample redress for the aggrieved
parties. Balked in this attempt to interfere, and
exasperated at the reply of Governor Cass, the British commander thereupon issued a proclamation of-
fering a reward of five hundred dollars for the ap-
prehension of the murderer. Cass promptly issued
a counter proclamation, requiring all citizens of the
Territory of Michigan to repel by force any attempt
which might be made to apprehend any person within
the Territory by virtue of the British proclamation
or any other process issued by any other authority
than that of the United States or the Michigan
Territory.[245] Needless to say the offender was not
turned over to the British for punishment.   The
position of the English was so flagrantly untenable
and so plainly assumed for the purpose of influencing
the Indians and appearing as the public champion of
the Indian cause that the Governor's rebuke of such
unwarrantable interference must be regarded as very
moderate.

On another occasion an armed British vessel intercepted and boarded several American schooners and examined their crews and lading for the purpose of taking off alleged British deserters.   Governor Cass promptly notified the commanding officer of the British vessel that such an arrogant and imperious encroachment upon the rights of American citizens was without justification.   "In an aggression like this," he said, "the government of the United States can alone determine what course the honor and interest of the nation requires should be taken.   But until their decision shall be made known upon the subject, it becomes my duty to remonstrate against a practice for which the laws of nations afford no pretense; which is inconsistent with the relations existing between our respective governments; and the continuance of which must be attended with serious and important consequences."[246]   The Governor's firm attitude seems to have had the desired effect, for no further complaints were heard.   The government approved the position Cass had taken, and stood ready to resort to war to uphold the right of liberty and freedom against foreign interference.

In 1823 the Territory of Michigan entered upon a second stage of organization.   It should be noted, however, that this change did not introduce the second grade of Territorial government as provided by the Ordinance, since the legislative power was vested in a single body — the Legislative Council.   Congress by special act provided that the Legislative Council

was to be composed of nine members chosen by the
President, with the consent of the Senate, out of
eighteen candidates selected by the people of the Territory.[247]   Moreover, an act in 1825 contained some
of the most important amendments to the plan of the
Ordinance that had yet been attempted: it undertook to prevent any further differences in the matter
of laying out townships by stipulating that the Governor and Legislative Council should have the right
to divide the Territory into townships and provide
for their incorporation and mode of government.
The Governor's right to appoint all civil officers was
continued, but the consent of the Legislative Council
was made necessary in confirmation of all such appointments.[248]

This last provision made the Governor's appointive power more nearly analogous to that exercised by the President of the United States, and
constituted an important constitutional check upon
his authority.   On the other hand, the Governor had
gained a decided advantage by the right to control
the organization of townships.   St. Clair had in-
sisted only on the right to lay out the counties and
townships — a bare right of designation which was
disputed by the legislature.   Under the act of 1825
the Governor had the power of allotment and also
the right to form the plan of local government. This
power was checked by the approval of the Council
it is true, but the Governor still had the initiative,

which, even with such a check, is an important prerogative in the hands of a discreet executive.

In 1827 the right of electing the members of the
Legislative Council was given to the people of the
Territory [249]— an extension of the franchise which
followed naturally as a result of the increasing population, and which was in line with the general policy of altering the Territorial government to suit
the development of the country.

The first elective legislature of the Territory of
Michigan met on June 7, 1824, in the old Council
House at Detroit; and there Governor Cass delivered his first message.[250] It was a careful exposi-
tion of the needs of the Territory, and one of the
strongest recommendations was that the laws be
revised and codified. It is interesting to note in this
connection that many of the enactments of the Northwest Territory still persisted in Michigan. Persons
practicing witchcraft were punished by a fine not to
exceed fifty dollars or by imprisonment for not more
than three months; the care of the poor was sold by
the sheriff to the best bidder; while imprisonment
for debt was retained in the Territory until 1822 and
in a modified form for many years thereafter. Persons guilty of petty offences, upon the order of a
Justice of the Peace, were publicly whipped, and
their services for a period of not more than three
months sold at auction to the highest bidder.[251] It
is said that not until 1831 was the old, notorious
whipping-post that stood in the market-place at De-

troit removed.[252] Many new and up-to-date laws
were in fact needed, but the Governor warned the
law-makers against hasty or ill-advised measures,
and urged that the laws be codified.

The Governor also recommended that a more
popular system of local government be adopted.
The county government had since 1820 consisted
merely of three commissioners for each county, appointed by the Governor.[253] In accordance with the
recommendation of Cass, it was provided in 1825
that these county commissioners should be elected
by the people.[254] No better illustration is needed
to reveal the sincere devotion of Governor Cass to
the interests of the people of the Territory. Moreover, he continued to urge a further extension of
popular rights and privileges, and it was largely
through his influence that Congress passed the act
of 1827, which provided that the members of the
Legislative Council should be elected by the people,
abolished the county commissioner system, and
established the town meeting for the election of
township and county officers.[255] Each township
now selected one supervisor and all these met together as the county board. Thus the township-
county system of local government became established in the Territory.[256] Governor Cass was largely instrumental in shaping the local government of Michigan, and in enlarging the franchise and the participation of the people in the administration of the
government during Territorial days.

The extension of land rights and the discovery of rich mineral and other natural resources led to a rapid increase in the population of the Territory; and so quite naturally Governor Cass turned his attention to the needs of its material development. He planned the building of one or two government roads to facilitate trade and travel, as well as the improvement of important highways throughout the Territory; and he secured aid from time to time from the general government for these projects.[257] Under his wise administration the Territory grew strong and prosperous. By the year 1830 the census showed a population of over thirty thousand; while in industrial and civil development the Territory was almost ready for statehood.

The great task of Governor Cass was now accomplished, and the indifferent, alien, and inharmonious elements were assimilated into a genuine American community. Michigan was Americanized —a service for which not only Michigan but the whole United States owes Lewis Cass a debt of gratitude. The spirit of independence and self-government which he instilled into the people became one of the chief assets of Michigan in later years.

Thus through all the vicissitudes of frontier advancement, by a wise and vigorous administration of public affairs for a period of eighteen years, Governor Cass strengthened the foundation of the prosperity of the Territory of Michigan. In 1832 President Jackson selected Cass as his Secretary of War,

a position which afforded him a larger field in which
to exercise the broad statesmanship that made his
term as Governor one of the most notable in Territorial history in the United States.

When Governor Cass ended his term of office
in the Territory the question of the appointment of
new Territorial officers became a pertinent one.
President Jackson's newly inaugurated "spoils system" was now a feature in National politics, and the
Territorial offices were luscious plums for his friends
and politicians in the doubtful States. It was mainly
on these grounds that the President appointed John
T. Mason of Virginia as the new Secretary for the
Territory of Michigan. Mason decided to go abroad,
however, and requested that his son, Stevens T.
Mason, be appointed in his place. This request was
complied with, and the boy not yet of age took charge
of this important office.[258]

By a queer chain of circumstances the persons
appointed by the President as Governor from time
to time during the remainder of the Territorial period spent but little if any time in the Territory, and
so the boy Secretary as Acting Governor performed
the duties of the executive office.[259] Fortunately he
carried on the affairs of the Territory with considerable ability.

In 1834, just as young Mason assumed the duties of his office, the great region west of the Mississippi and north of the State of Missouri was rescued
from the state of constitutional oblivion to which it

had so long been consigned and attached to the Territory of Michigan for purposes of local government.[260]   Little attention, however, was paid to this vast western region just opened to immigration, fringed with two or three rudimentary settlements and dotted with a few lonely settlers' cabins — a region far away from the scenes of activity in the Territory, as yet little known, and thought of only as a desolate wilderness.   Moreover, the officers and people of the Territory were so engrossed in the excitement of a boundary dispute with Ohio, and in the political agitations connected with the preparations for statehood, that they had little time or thought for their great western domains.   It is manifest, therefore, that with the exception of a few legislative acts the direct influence of the Michigan government upon that part of the country was small, and that the frontiersmen across the great river were left very much to themselves as far as the authorities of the Michigan Territory were concerned.

When the boundary dispute with Ohio arose the Governor defended the cause of Michigan with so much ardor and ability that ''his administration became as popular as at first it had been obnoxious.''[261] Experience in office had also fitted him for its duties; and it is an interesting fact that Stevens T. Mason was elected first Governor under the provisional State government in 1835.   It was he who piloted the Territorial and provisional governments through the peculiar entanglements that marked the transition from Territory to State.[262]

The trouble which Michigan experienced in forming a State constitution was not caused by any lack of inclination on the part of the people, but by the difficulty of securing satisfactory terms of admission.[263] The experience of the Territorial period had trained the people in independent thinking. Michigan had been the border battlefield over which had surged French, English, and American forces in their attempts to control the country. And now that under the guidance of Governor Cass they had thrown off old prejudices and customs, the people were strong and vigorous Americans, ready to fight for their rights and to stand solidly together at any cost.

The broad statesmanship of Lewis Cass is the distinctive feature of the Territorial history of Michigan. It was indeed a great work to Americanize the Territory of Michigan, and the success with which it was accomplished is additional evidence of the wisdom of the policy that placed strong men with large discretionary powers at the head of our Territorial governments.

GOVERNORS DODGE AND DOTY AND THE TERRITORY OF WISCONSIN

While the Territory of Michigan was wrangling with the State of Ohio over boundaries and the people were wondering whether they were still a Territory or had become a State within the Union, the inhabitants of the region west of Lake Michigan began to feel the need of a government of their own. Indeed, there had for some time been agitation for a separate Territorial government. The matter was taken up by the Legislative Council and a memorial was sent to Congress requesting that all the country west of Lake Michigan, not included in the new State that was about to be admitted, should be organized as a separate Territory. The result was that on April 20, 1836, the Territory of Wisconsin was established.[264]

The Organic Act of the new Territory was modeled upon the fundamental principles of the Ordinance of 1787. The Governor was still the dominating power in the government, with practically the same powers and duties as his predecessors.

An important change, however, was made in the method of legislation. Instead of the Governor and Judges being constituted the first law-making body,

the powers of legislation were from the first vested
in the Governor and a Legislative Assembly.   The
Assembly consisted of a House of Representatives
of twenty-six members elected for two years, and a
Council of thirteen members elected for four years.
The experience of Indiana, Illinois, and Michigan
was bearing fruit. As an integral part of the Territory of Michigan, Wisconsin had developed a capacity for self-government which rendered the preparatory first stage unnecessary. Whether this fact
consciously influenced the framers of the Organic
Act or not, it is at any rate certain that the democratic tendencies that were shaping National politics
were beginning to be reflected in the laws for the
formation of Territories.

General Henry Dodge was appointed as the first
Governor of the Territory, and John S. Horner was
commissioned Secretary. At Mineral Point on July
4, 1836, as one of the incidents of the holiday celebra-
tion, the Governor and other officials took the oath
of office and were duly installed as officers of the
Territory.

Henry Dodge brought to the Territorial governorship a wide experience in frontier affairs. He
had grown up in the wilderness and knew the needs
of the frontier; his long and varied official service
provided him with a fund of experience upon which
he could draw when difficult problems presented
themselves for solution. He was a man of strong
physique, forceful and decisive in his words and ac-

tions, and dignified in appearance. His early education had been scanty and mostly confined to the
rough school of experience; but he made up in rugged
perseverance and in strength of intellect what he
lacked in schooling. In politics he was a thorough-
going Democrat; and he was popular with the
masses, who always seemed to have great confidence
in him.[265]

Among the six counties which had been laid out
while Wisconsin was still a part of the Territory of
Michigan, the Governor proceeded to apportion the
thirteen Councillors and the twenty-six Representa-
tievs ''as nearly equal as practicable''. This proved
a delicate task. Crawford County, not having one-
thirteenth of the whole population, was left without
representation in the Council. In his endeavor to
be fair the Governor allotted to Crawford County
two members of the House of Representatives — all,
if not more than it was strictly entitled to.[266] But
the people of Crawford County were not satisfied,
contending that each county should have at least one
Councillor. A public indignation meeting was held
and an emphatic protest was registered against the
apportionment.[267]

By proclamation Governor Dodge named October 10, 1836, as the day for electing members of the
Council and House of Representatives and a Delegate to Congress. The proclamation further directed that the Legislative Assembly should convene
at Belmont in Iowa County on October 25.[268] Craw-

ford County proceeded to elect a member of the
Council as well as two Representatives, and demanded that the Governor declare the election
valid.[269] This the Governor refused to do, and in his
proclamation announcing the results of the election
he ignored the Councilor from Crawford County.[270]
The Legislative Assembly, moreover, stood by the
Governor in refusing to give the protesting county
a seat in the Council, and thus the matter ended.

Governor Dodge's first message to the Legislative Assembly was a concise and businesslike presen-
tation of the needs of the Territory.[271] The organization of a judicial system and the division of the
Territory into judicial districts was the first subject
considered. Then came a recommendation that a
memorial be forwarded to Congress on the subject
of extending the right of preëmption to actual settlers. He thought that, considering the condition of
the United States Treasury, there was no necessity
for selling public land to the actual settler at the
price of one dollar and a quarter an acre, and that in
justice the price should be reduced and graduated
according to the value of the land.

The question of internal improvements also received much emphasis. Governor Dodge recommended that Congress be asked to make appropriations for the removal of obstructions in the upper
Mississippi, for the construction of harbors and
light-houses on Lake Michigan, and for the improvement of the navigation of the Fox River.   An enter-

prising company acting under a charter from the Territory of Michigan had already commenced a canal between the Wisconsin and Fox rivers. The further improvement of the Fox River would thus provide water communication between Lake Michigan and the Mississippi, and would greatly facilitate commerce and the transportation of troops and munitions of war in case of necessity. The improvement of the navigation of the Rock River would in the same way, he thought, open up a large region; while a railroad from Lake Michigan to the Mississippi would repay donations of land by the government for that purpose.

Governor Dodge further recommended that Congress be asked to donate one township of land for the establishment of an academy. Believing that in times of peace preparations should be made for war, he suggested the passage of a law organizing a company of sixty volunteer mounted riflemen for each county in the Territory and that these troops be properly equipped, drilled, and inspected. Finally, Governor Dodge showed his practical wisdom by announcing that in regard to the location of the permanent seat of government of the Territory, he would give his assent to whatever the members of the legislature thought would best promote the public good. A number of town sites had been laid out by speculators each of whom was trying to make his particular city the metropolis of the Territory. The strife for supremacy was very bitter, and the

Governor would have gained nothing by taking sides in the quarrel.

Governor Dodge's first message is worthy of detailed examination, since it reflects the dominant ideas in the new Territory. The Legislative Assembly proceeded to carry out many of the Governor's recommendations, and the crowning achievment of the first session was the location of the capital of the Territory at Madison, the newly platted town so charmingly situated within encircling lakes.[272]

The Territorial legislature met for its second session on November 6, 1837, at Burlington in Des Moines County on the west bank of the Mississippi River. In his message Governor Dodge emphasized the necessity for preëmption laws and for a more thoroughly equipped militia. He called attention to various subjects upon which legislation was needed, and considered at some length the dispute over the boundary line between the State of Missouri and the Territory of Wisconsin.[273]

A number of important laws were enacted by the legislature at its second session — perhaps the most noteworthy being an act abolishing imprisonment for debt. Several universities and seminaries were established, and Congress was asked to make a special appropriation for a University of the Territory of Wisconsin to be located at Madison. Considerable time was also devoted to enacting legislation for the organization of new counties and for

locating county seats.[274]   Indeed, Governor Dodge
seemed to think that the Assembly was carrying this
line of legislation too far, for in his first veto message he considered at some length his reasons for
returning a bill fixing the boundaries of several counties and establishing the seats of justice.

The changes of the location of two county seats
were considered by Dodge to be particularly objec-
tionable: in one case he declared that he could not
think of a single good reason for the proposed removal.   "In a territory like ours", he said, "great
care and caution should be exercised in the location
of the seats of justice in the first place; and where
settlements are formed on the faith of our acts,
changes should not, in my opinion, be made without
the prospect of some substantial benefit to the people, and upon their wish unequivocally expressed to
that effect."   And he pointedly remarked that a provision for a direct vote of the people upon such questions would meet with his approval.[275]   It was fortunate that the Governor put a check upon the legislature in this matter, for the prevalence of speculators and town-boomers stimulated an unnecessary
activity in the location of county seats.

The details of the remaining years of Governor
Dodge's administration need not be related.   In general it may be said that the policies already outlined
were followed throughout the period.   Dodge, perhaps more than any of the other Territorial Governors of the Old Northwest, took an active interest

in legislation. Through messages and by more direct and personal influences he secured the enactment of a large number of laws which were highly
beneficial to the Territory. While he negotiated a
number of Indian treaties, his duties as Superintendent of Indian Affairs were not nearly so burdensome
as had been the duties of his predecessors in this
respect. Comparative freedom from Indian troubles
and from perplexing problems of settling land dis-
putes and relieving distress allowed Dodge to devote
himself very largely to civil administration.

On the whole the administration of Governor
Dodge was peaceful and successful. He had the remarkable faculty of insisting upon his prerogatives
and of securing compliance with his wishes without
arousing antagonism. As a result much permanent
good was accomplished and the Territory prospered
under his wise and efficient management of affairs.

In 1841 President Tyler removed Henry Dodge
for political reasons and appointed James Duane
Doty to the office of Governor of the Territory of
Wisconsin.

Governor Doty had served in various official
capacities in the Territory of Michigan, and when
appointed to the governorship he was Delegate to
Congress from the Territory of Wisconsin. He was,
therefore, well acquainted with the needs and conditions of the Territory. In private life he seems to
have been a man of genial and pleasing personality,
and it has been said that he was never defeated in

a contest for an elective office.[276]   But in his official
capacity Doty was aggressive and set in his ways,
and he was so intolerant of opposition that he made
many enemies.   He was so impulsive and at times
his unreasonable passion carried him to such extremes that it impaired his usually sound judgment.
Consequently his administration was the stormiest
in the history of the Territory.[277]

The Governor began sowing the seeds of discord
the moment he assumed office, by asserting in his inaugural address that no law of the Territory was
effective until expressly approved by Congress.   He
then proceeded to disregard such laws as ran counter
to his ideas of what was necessary in given cases.[278]
This was a usurpation of power which the Legislative Assembly naturally resented.   Doty also ir-
ritated the legislature by denying the right of that
body to appoint certain officials.

When the legislature convened in 1842 the Governor took further occasion to assert his authority.
It had been provided by law that the annual session
of the legislature should commence on the first Mon-
day in December.   On December 5, 1842, the members organized and waited upon the Governor, but
to their chagrin he informed them that, "not con-
ceiving that the legislative assembly had authority
by law to meet at the present time, he had no communication to make to them".[279]   Doty gave as his
reason that there had been no appropriation to cover
the expenses of a session of the legislature. A bitter

controversy ensued and it was not until March 6, 1843, that the legislature finally convened with the Governor's approval.[280] Whether the Governor was animated in this case by spite, desire to display his authority, or simply through obstinacy, his conduct in any event seems indefensible.

From this time on there was constant warfare between Governor Doty and the legislature. The question of statehood in 1843, the appointment of a Treasurer for the Territory two years earlier, and various other subjects furnished opportunities for clash of opinions. Moreover, Doty had so long been interested in land speculations that it was difficult to persuade a certain class of the people that he was not using his office to further his own ends. His financial policies were continually attacked in the newspapers, and it has been said that he never entirely cleared himself from some of the charges in relation to his financial dealings.[281] It is probable, however, that political considerations and the insecure banking system of the Territory were responsible for much of the opposition to Governor Doty.

Finally, in 1844 the President removed Doty and appointed Nathaniel P. Tallmadge, a New York politician, in his place. Tallmadge had been a member of the New York legislature and had held a seat in the United States Senate. He was a man of considerable ability, and during the one year in which he held the office of Governor of the Territory of Wis-

consin his relations with the legislature were friendly and harmonious.

Political changes were now beginning to be considered in the light of necessities. Governor Tallmadge had scarcely become accustomed to the duties
of his office before the accession of James K. Polk to
the presidency in 1845 made another change necessary, according to political custom; and on April 8,
1845, the President reappointed Henry Dodge as
Governor. Dodge had been serving as Delegate to
Congress and with the benefit of this added experience he resumed the duties of the governorship.

The Territory had been growing rapidly in population, and by this time the people began to desire
larger measures of self-government. In April, 1846,
the question of the advisability of forming a State
government was put to a vote, and the result showed
that the people were overwhelmingly in favor of the
change. After one unsuccessful attempt a constitution was adopted, and on May 29, 1848, Wisconsin
was duly admitted into the Union as a State.[282]

Perhaps the most noticeable feature of the Territorial period in Wisconsin is the growing interest
in politics on the part of the people. Governors
changed as the party in power in the Nation changed,
and the spirit of partisan politics began to influence
the conduct of affairs in the Territory. It is chiefly
in this respect that the history of the Territory of
Wisconsin differs from that of the earlier Territories
in the Old Northwest. Although the Governor still

remained the dominating influence in the Territory, he was shorn of his power in many minor details and a tendency towards decentralization is clearly discernible.

NOTES AND REFERENCES

NOTES AND REFERENCES

CHAPTER I

[1] An excellent account of the long struggle between France and England for supremacy in the New World will be found in the writings of Francis Parkman.

[2] See Macdonald's *Select Charters and Other Documents Illustrative of American History, 1606-1775*, pp. 261-266; and Winsor's *The Mississippi Basin*, p. 419.

[3] *The Annual Register*, 1763, Part I, p. 211. See also Winsor's *The Westward Movement*, p. 2.

[4] For good, brief accounts of the Revolution in the West see Roosevelt's *The Winning of the West* (Statesman Edition), Vol. II, pp. 1-175; and Thwaites's *How George Rogers Clark Won the Northwest*. The *Draper Collection of Manuscripts* in the library of The State Historical Society of Wisconsin at Madison is rich in materials on this period.

[5] McLaughlin's *Lewis Cass*, pp. 1-33. It would seem, however, that location and other natural conditions also exerted a great influence in retarding American settlement along the northern border. For instance, Minnesota lagged many years behind Iowa. The line of settlement appears to have been a determining factor, but doubtless many other causes contributed to the result.

[6] See *American State Papers, Foreign Relations*, Vol. I, for papers relating to Spain's control of the navigation

of the Mississippi River, and *American State Papers, Indian Affairs*, Vol. I, for papers dealing with Spanish attempts to incite the Indians to warfare against the United States. Ogg's *The Opening of the Mississippi* and Green's *The Spanish Conspiracy* are monographs dealing especially with this subject.

[7] For material dealing with the relations of the English with the Indians during the Revolutionary period see *American State Papers, Indian Affairs*, Vol. I; *The Haldimand Papers* in the *Collections and Researches Made by the Pioneer and Historical Society of the State of Michigan*, Vol. X; and the *Draper Collection of Manuscripts* in the library of the State Historical Society of Wisconsin at Madison.

[8] See McLaughlin's *The Western Posts and the British Debts* in the *Annual Report of the American Historical Association*, 1894, pp. 412-444.

[9] Roosevelt's *The Winning of the West* (Statesman Edition), Vol. I, pp. 38-42; Vol. III, pp. 325-328. Great stress is rightly laid on this point, and it is reiterated and illustrated throughout the four volumes of Mr. Roosevelt's work. For interesting examples of the trend of this individualism in the Southwest consult also Turner's *Western State-Making in the Revolutionary Era* in *The American Historical Review*, Vol I, pp. 70, 251.

[10] In a note in Roosevelt's *The Winning of the West* (Statesman Edition), Vol. III, pp. 329-330; it is stated on evidence from manuscripts in the Department of State at Washington, D. C., that in 1787 there were 103 adult male Americans in Vincennes and 137 in the Illinois villages. In the *Manuscript Papers and Records of the Territories*, Vol. I, at Washington, there appears a list of heads of fam-

ilies settled at Fort Vincennes before 1783, prepared by Winthrop Sargent, Secretary of the Northwest Territory. This list includes 121 heads of families, with 23 widows and one deserted wife, making a total of 145. Winsor says there were "perhaps a thousand French, and they numbered four to one American."— Winsor's *The Westward Movement*, p. 275.

[11] See Turner's *Rise of the New West*, pp. 67-83.

CHAPTER II

[12] This act was passed in October, 1778. — Hening's *Statutes at Large*, Vol. IX, p. 552. In May, 1780, the legislature of Virginia amended the act and provided that it should continue in force for another year.— Hening's *Statutes at Large*, Vol. X, p. 303. So as a matter of fact that form of government was valid only until 1781, since it was not again renewed. It was actually enforced in the Northwest, however, for several years subsequent to that time.

The present discussion of the government of this country as a county under Virginia follows very closely Boyd's *The County of Illinois* in *The American Historical Review*, Vol. IV, pp. 623-635; but the point of view in this book is somewhat different from that of Mr. Boyd's article.

[13] Boyd's *The County of Illinois* in *The American Historical Review*, Vol. IV, p. 624.

[14] *John Todd's Record-Book* in the *Chicago Historical Society's Collection*, Vol. IV, pp. 289-294; Henry's *Patrick Henry*, Vol. III, pp. 212-216; and Mason's *Col. John Todd's Record-Book* in the *Fergus Historical Series*, No. 12, p. 51.

[15] Green's *Historic Families of Kentucky*, pp. 210-211.

¹⁶ *Draper Collection — Clark MSS*, Vol. 60, p. 4, State Historical Society of Wisconsin. There are sixty-four large bound volumes of the George Rogers Clark papers.

¹⁷ Letter from George Rogers Clark to George Mason, quoted in Thwaites's *How George Rogers Clark Won the Northwest*, p. 64.

¹⁸ Nine judges were elected at Kaskaskia, seven at Cahokia, and nine at Vincennes.—*John Todd's Record-Book* in the *Chicago Historical Society's Collection*, Vol. IV, p. 295.

¹⁹ See Moses's *Illinois, Historical and Statistical,* Vol. I, p. 160.

²⁰ *John Todd's Record-Book* in the *Chicago Historical Society's Collection,* Vol. IV, pp. 304, 308-314.

²¹ *American State Papers, Public Lands*, Vol. II, p. 102; and *John Todd's Record-Book* in the *Chicago Historical Society's Collection*, Vol. IV, p. 301.

²² *Draper Collection — Clark MSS*, Vol. 49, Nos. 78, 79; and *John Todd's Record-Book* in the *Chicago Historical Society's Collection*, Vol. IV, pp. 305, 306.

²³ Letters from the Illinois County are full of this dissatisfaction.— *Draper Collection — Clark MSS*, Vol. 49, Nos. 71, 72, 73, 78; *John Todd Papers* in the *Chicago Historical Society's Collection*, Vol. IV, p. 319; and Palmer's *Calendar of Virginia State Papers*, Vol. I, pp. 379, 460.

²⁴ Palmer's *Calendar of Virginia State Papers*, Vol. I, p. 379.

²⁵ It would appear from Demunbrunt's petition to the Virginia government that he had been appointed by Colonel Winston as commandant of the village of Kaskaskia.— Pal-

mer and McRae's *Calendar of Virginia State Papers,* Vol.
V, p. 408.   The endorsement in the record-book, however,
reads: ''THIMOTHÉ DEMUNBRUNT, Lt. Comd't. Par inter-
im''.—*John Todd's Record-Book* in the *Chicago Historical Society's Collection,* Vol. IV, p. 316.

[26] See letter from John Dodge, Indian Agent at Fort
Jefferson, to John Todd in June, 1780.— *Draper Collection
— Clark MSS,* Vol. 29, No. 36; and letter from Winston to
Todd, October 24, 1780.— Palmer's *Calendar of Virginia
State Papers,* Vol. I, p. 381.

[27] *Draper Collection — Clark MSS,* Vol. 23, p. 228;
Vol. 50, Nos. 5, 70.

[28] See above, note 12.

[29] *Draper Collection — Clark MSS,* Vol. 60, pp. 262-
263.

[30] Carbonneaux had come on a mission to represent the
condition of the Illinois country, and made the statement
to Walker Daniel, who under date of ''New Holland, Feb.
3, 1783'', reported it to the Board of Commissioners for the
Western Department of Virginia.— *Draper Collection —
Clark MSS,* Vol. 60, pp. 211-212.

CHAPTER III

[31] For instance see *Journals of the American Congress:
From 1774 to 1788* (Way and Gideon Edition), Vol. IV,
pp. 341, 574, 575, 688, 811.

[32] A concise account of the early attempts to form a
government for the Old Northwest, written by Peter Force
and consisting largely of extracts from the *Journals of Congress,* may be found in Smith's *The St. Clair Papers,* Vol.
II, pp. 603-608.

[33] See Cutler's *Life, Journals and Correspondence of Rev. Manasseh Cutler,* Vol. I, Ch. IV.

[34] *Journals of the American Congress: From 1774 to 1788* (Way and Gideon Edition), Vol. IV, pp. 751-754. The text of the Ordinance of 1787, together with a list of references, will be found in convenient form in Shambaugh's *Documentary Material Relating to the History of Iowa,* Vol. I, pp. 47-55.

[35] For discussions on the authorship of the Ordinance, see *The Works of Daniel Webster* (Twentieth Edition), Vol. III, pp. 263-264; Cutler's *Life, Journals and Correspondence of Rev. Manasseh Cutler,* Vol. I, pp. 343, 350; Poole's *Dr. Cutler and the Ordinance of 1787* in the *North American Review,* Vol. CXXII, pp. 229-265; Farrand's *The Legislation of Congress for the Government of the Organized Territories of the United States,* p. 9; Barrett's *Evolution of the Ordinance of 1787;* and Hinsdale's *The Old Northwest,* pp. 263-279.

[36] See appropriation acts in *United States Statutes at Large,* Vol. I. The regular items were included in the yearly appropriation bills, and special appropriations were made from time to time as needed.

[37] Article 5 of the Articles of Compact in the Ordinance.

[38] See decision of the Supreme Court of the United States on this point in the case of Strader *v.* Graham, 10 Howard 82. See also Jameson's *A Treatise on Constitutional Conventions,* p. 179.

[39] *United States Statutes at Large,* Vol. I, p. 50.

CHAPTER IV

[40] See Greene's *The Provincial Governor in the English Colonies of North America* in the *Harvard Historical Studies,* Vol. VII, pp. 177-195.

[41] Act of September 11, 1789.— *United States Statutes at Large,* Vol. I, p. 67.   This act also fixed the salary of the Secretary of the Territory at $750 per year, and that of each of the three Judges at $800.   The Governor's salary remained unchanged until 1836, when the Governor of the Territory of Wisconsin was given for his services as Governor and Superintendent of Indian Affairs $2,500 per year in accordance with a provision of the Organic Act.

[42] See appropriation acts of 1791, 1797, 1809, 1825, and 1835.— *United States Statutes at Large,* Vol. I, pp. 226, 500; Vol. II, p. 523; Vol. IV, pp. 189, 766.

[43] *United States Statutes at Large,* Vol. I, pp. 54, 333, 539.

[44] Smith's *The Liberty and Free Soil Parties in the Northwest* in the *Harvard Historical Studies,* Vol. VI, p. 1.

[45] See Reinsch's *Colonial Government,* pp. 271, 311.

CHAPTER V

[46] *Journals of the American Congress: From 1774 to 1788* (Way and Gideon Edition), p. 786.

[47] Burnet's *Notes on the Early Settlement of the North-Western Territory,* pp. 374, 375, 378.

[48] Winsor's *The Westward Movement,* p. 302.

[49] Darlington's *Journal and Letters of Col. John May, of Boston Relative to Two Journeys to the Ohio Country in 1788 and '89,* p. 68.

[50] Darlington's *Journal and Letters of Col. John May, of Boston Relative to Two Journeys to the Ohio Country in 1788 and '89,* pp. 83, 85.   St. Clair's inaugural address may be found in Smith's *The St. Clair Papers,* Vol. II, pp. 53-56.

[51] Smith's *The St. Clair Papers,* Vol. II, pp. 78-79.

[52] For these recommendations see Smith's *The St. Clair Papers,* Vol. II, pp. 61-63.   The militia law is found in Chase's *The Statutes of Ohio,* Vol. I, pp. 92-93.

[53] Chase's *The Statutes of Ohio,* Vol. I, pp. 92-103. These laws covered such subjects as the militia, the system of courts, oaths of office, crimes and punishments, the regulation of marriages, the appointment of coroners, and the time of commencing civil actions and instituting criminal prosecutions.

[54] *United States Statutes at Large,* Vol. I, pp. 285-286.

[55] Chase's *The Statutes of Ohio,* Vol. I, pp. 19-20.

[56] Smith's *The St. Clair Papers,* Vol. I, p. 148.

[57] Chase's *The Statutes of Ohio,* Vol. I, pp. 94-96.

[58] "I saw a record proceeding at Prairie du Rocher against a colored man for the murder of a hog.   At that day no prosecuting attorney attended the court, and I presume the grand-jury found the form of an indictment in some book, for murder, and applied it to the negro and the hog.   It was malicious mischief in destroying the hog, which I presume was the offence the grand-jury was investigating.   The same equitable justice may have been done under the indictment for murder, as if it were one for malicious mischief and prosecuted by the ablest attorneys in the country.''— Reynolds's *The Pioneer History of Illinois,* p. 181.

[59] Smith's *The St. Clair Papers,* Vol. II, pp. 131, 165, 166.

[60] Chase's *The Statutes of Ohio,* Vol. I, pp. 107-109.

[61] Chase's *The Statutes of Ohio,* Vol. I, pp. 344-346.

[62] Letter of July 31, 1788.— Smith's *The St. Clair Papers,* Vol. II, pp. 69-72.

[63] Letter from St. Clair to Judges Parsons and Varnum, August 7, 1788.— Smith's *The St. Clair Papers,* Vol. II, p. 74.

[64] See *United States Statutes at Large,* Vol. I, p. 266. The following extract from the *Cincinnati Advertiser* of November 2, 1819, is characteristic of Judge Symmes: "I declare the earth to be hollow, and habitable within; and constituted of a number of concentric spheres, the poles of which are open twelve or sixteen degrees. I pledge my life in support of this truth, and am ready to explore the concave, if the world will aid and support me in the undertaking. JNO. CLEVES SYMMES."— *Draper Collection — Papers of John C. Symmes,* Vol. I, unclassified.

[65] Letter dated August 24, 1791.— *Draper Collection — Papers of John C. Symmes,* Vol. I, No. 3.

[66] "I believe it an incontrovertible truth," he wrote, "that a large and respectable part of the people will never be contented while you hold the reins of government: — If therefore you have the interest of the people of this territory truly at heart, as you say you have, you will surely now let fall the curtain to your administration".— Letter from John C. Symmes to Arthur St. Clair, November 29, 1800.— *Draper Collection — Papers of John C. Symmes,* Vol. I, No. 4.

[67] Smith's *The St. Clair Papers,* Vol. II, pp. 68, 73.

[68] On February 12, 1795, the House of Representatives adopted a resolution disapproving of the laws enacted by the Governor and Judges of the Northwest Territory in 1792.— *Annals of Congress,* 2nd Session, 3rd Congress, pp. 721, 825, 830, 1214, 1223, 1227. See also Howard's *An Introduction to the Local Constitutional History of the United States,* Vol. I, p. 409, note.

[69] *United States Statutes at Large,* Vol. I, p. 286.

[70] Chase's *The Statutes of Ohio,* Vol. I, pp. 211-212.

[71] *Maxwell's Code* (1796). The same laws are to be found in Chase's *The Statutes of Ohio,* Vol. I, pp. 138-204.

[72] In Smith's *The St. Clair Paper's,* Vol. I, p. 148, the statement is made that in September, 1788, there were 132 people on the Ohio. Roosevelt states that there were about 4,000 inhabitants in the French villages in the Illinois country. Detroit, which was an old settlement, had a population of perhaps 2,000, including the territory immediately adjoining.— Roosevelt's *The Winning of the West* (Statesman Edition), Vol. I, pp. 49, 51. Detroit, however, was far removed from the direct influence of the Governor.

[73] Smith's *The St. Clair Papers,* Vol. I, p. 192.

[74] Governor St. Clair in his report to the Secretary of State on February 18, 1791, said: "Every public act and communication, of what kind soever, I was myself obliged to translate into French; and having no person to assist me, it made the business extremely troublesome and laborious."— *American State Papers, Public Lands,* Vol. I, p. 20.

[75] Smith's *The St. Clair Papers,* Vol. II, p. 32.

[76] See Green's *The Spanish Conspiracy,* and Ogg's

The Opening of the Mississippi. See also correspondence concerning the Kentucky expedition against the Spanish on the Mississippi.— *American State Papers, Foreign Affairs,* Vol. I, pp. 454-460.

[77] Winsor's *The Westward Movement,* pp. 306-308.

[78] *American State Papers, Indian Affairs,* Vol. I, contains numerous documents bearing on this point. See also Burnet's *Notes on the Early Settlement of the North-Western Territory,* pp. 164-167, 176-182; and Smith's *The St. Clair Papers,* Vol. II, p. 41.

[79] St. Clair's report of February 18, 1791, contains a review of the whole situation.— *American State Papers, Public Lands,* Vol. I, pp. 18-20.

[80] Roosevelt's *The Winning of the West* (Statesman Edition), Vol. III, p. 391. In July, 1788, St. Clair complained that the government of the State of New York was interfering with the plans of the National government regarding the making of a treaty with the Six Nations.— Smith's *The St. Clair Papers,* Vol. II, p. 49.

[81] *Secret Journals of the Acts and Proceedings of Congress,* Vol. I, pp. 276-279.

[82] Smith's *The St. Clair Papers,* Vol. II; and *American State Papers, Indian Affairs,* Vol. I, pp. 57, 58, 83-106, 121. For Indian treaties negotiated by St. Clair, see *United States Statutes at Large,* Vol. VII.

[83] Winsor's *The Westward Movement,* p. 429.

[84] The committee of the House of Representatives, in their inquiry into the cause of the defeat, freed Governor St. Clair from blame.— *Annals of Congress,* 2nd Congress, pp. 1106-1113, 1309-1317. St. Clair's report of the defeat

is found in *American State Papers, Indian Affairs*, Vol. I, pp. 136-138.   Good accounts of the battle are given in Captain Newman's journal of the St. Clair campaign in the *Draper Collection — Frontier Wars MSS*, Vol. IV, pp. 101-131, and in other papers in the same collection.

[85] "Meanwhile every one was busy seeking where to lay the blame.   The Antifederal sheets declared the disaster was due to the Bank and the Funding bill. . . . The people put the blame on St. Clair, and, as he passed through the villages on his return home, came in crowds to hiss him and taunt him with jeers.   The Secretary of War thought the defeat was to be ascribed to the rawness of the troops. The committee of the House of Representatives laid it to the lateness of the season and the negligence of Hodgdon, the quartermaster, and the dishonesty of William Duer, the contractor for army supplies.   But there were those who thought the month of November and a lazy officer had nothing to do with an Indian surprise."— McMaster's *A History of the People of the United States*, Vol. II, p. 47.

[86] *United States Statutes at Large*, Vol. I, pp. 285-286.

[87] Burnet's *Notes on the Early Settlement of the North-Western Territory*, pp. 64-70.

[88] *United States Statutes at Large*, Vol. I, pp. 285-286.

[89] Letter from St. Clair to Thomas Jefferson, December 14, 1794.— Smith's *The St. Clair Papers*, Vol. II, pp. 332-333.

[90] Chase's *The Statutes of Ohio*, Vol. I, p. 26.

[91] Chase's *The Statutes of Ohio*, Vol. I, p. 187.

[92] Chase's *The Statutes of Ohio*, Vol. I, pp. 97-101.

[93] Chase's *The Statutes of Ohio*, Vol. I, p. 143.   Con-

gress later modified this act somewhat.— *United States Statutes at Large,* Vol. I, p. 482.

[94] Chase's *The Statutes of Ohio,* Vol. I, p. 190. This law was taken from an act which was passed by the colonial legislature of Virginia, and which had long since been repealed when it was adopted by the codifiers. Technically, therefore, the law was void.

[95] Smith's *The St. Clair Papers,* Vol. II, pp. 441-442.

[96] Speech of Governor St. Clair before the first Territorial legislature, December 19, 1799.— Smith's *The St. Clair Papers,* Vol. II, pp. 477-478.

[97] Hinsdale's *The Old Northwest,* p. 300.

[98] Burnet's *Notes on the Early Settlement of the North-Western Territory,* pp. 328-334; and Walker's *History of Athens County, Ohio,* p. 137.

[99] Ferris's *The States and Territories of the Great West,* p. 166.

[100] The letter, which is given in Smith's *The St. Clair Papers,* Vol. I, pp. 244-246, is as follows:

Department of State,
Washington, November 22, 1802.

ARTHUR ST. CLAIR, Esq.:

SIR:— The President observing, in an address lately delivered by you to the convention held at Chillicothe, an intemperance and indecorum of language toward the Legislature of the United States, and a disorganizing spirit and tendency of very evil example, and grossly violating the rules of conduct enjoined by your public station, determines that your commission of Governor of the North-western Territory shall cease on the receipt of this notification.

I am, etc.,
JAMES MADISON.

[101] Hinsdale's *The Old Northwest,* p. 312.

[102] *United States Statutes at Large,* Vol. II, p. 173.

[103] See the first Constitution of Ohio in Chase's *The Statutes of Ohio,* Vol. I, p. 75.

CHAPTER VI

[104] *United States Statutes at Large,* Vol. II, p. 58. This act went into force on July 4, 1800.

[105] *American State Papers, Miscellaneous,* Vol. I, p. 206.

[106] In an autobiographical sketch dated July 20, 1839, published in a local New York newspaper, Harrison stated that although his instructions allowed him to draw whatever money he desired for the administration of Indian affairs, he made it a practice to charge only for the time actually employed in a specific negotiation.— *Draper Collection — Harrison Papers,* Vol. I.   See also Harrison's letter to the editor of the Ohio Confederate, October 18, 1839, quoted in Burr's *The Life and Times of William Henry Harrison,* pp. 297-300.

[107] *American State Papers, Public Lands,* Vol. I, p. 93.

[108] *Laws of Indiana Territory,* 1801, pp. 5, 6.

[109] *Laws of Indiana Territory,* 1801, pp. 28-29.

[110] *Laws of Indiana Territory,* 1801, 1802, 1803; and Howard's *An Introduction to the Local Constitutional History of the United States,* p. 426.

[111] *Laws of Indiana Territory,* 1801, 1802, 1803.

[112] Dunn's *Indiana,* p. 295.

[113] See a letter from Judge Parke to Governor Posey, February 7, 1814, and a memorial to Congress from the legislature of the Indiana Territory, October 18, 1814.— Dillon's *A History of Indiana,* pp. 543-545.

[114] Act of February 24, 1815.— *United States Statutes at Large*, Vol. III, p. 213.

[115] Letter from Harrison to the editor of the *Ohio Confederate*, October 18, 1839, quoted in Burr's *The Life and Times of William Henry Harrison*, pp. 297-300.

[116] See *United States Statutes at Large*, Vol. VII.

[117] The average price paid for Indian lands in this region seems to have been less than one cent per acre. See letter from Henry Dearborn to James Robertson and Silas Dinsmore.— *American State Papers, Indian Affairs*, Vol. I, p. 700.

[118] Jefferson's message of January 30, 1808.— Richardson's *Messages and Papers of the Presidents*, Vol. I, pp. 438-439.

[119] See *Draper Collection — Harrison Papers* for letters and papers dealing with Harrison's management of Indian affairs. See also Dawson's *A Historical Narrative of the Civil and Military Services of Major-General William H. Harrison.*

[120] See Harrison's letter to Madison, January, 1802,— *American State Papers, Public Lands*, Vol. I, pp. 122-123.

[121] *United States Statutes at Large*, Vol. II, p. 277.

[122] For discussions of the land policy of the United States government see Donaldson's *The Public Domain;* and Sato's *History of the Land Question in the United States* in the *Johns Hopkins University Studies in Historical and Political Science*, Vol. IV. See *United States Statutes at Large*, Vol. II, p. 343, note, for a list of acts relating to public lands in Indiana.

[123] *American State Papers, Public Lands*, Vol. II, p.

102.   See also Davidson and Stuvé's *A Complete History of Illinois from 1673 to 1873,* pp. 235-239.

[124] Report of December 17, 1811.— *American State Papers, Public Lands,* Vol. II, p. 223.

[125] *American State Papers, Public Lands,* Vol. VI, p. 23.   Many of the Governor's grants were confirmed by Congress.— *United States Statutes at Large,* Vol. II, p. 447.

[126] *United States Statutes at Large,* Vol. II, p. 283.

[127] *United States Statutes at Large,* Vol. II, p. 331.

[128] *United States Statutes at Large,* Vol. II, p. 444.

[129] See *American State Papers, Public Lands,* Vol. I, pp. 68, 160; Smith's *The St. Clair Papers,* Vol. II, pp. 447, 451; and Dunn's *Indiana,* pp. 284-293, 297, 298, 368-370, for instances of such petitions.

[130] See *American State Papers, Public Lands,* Vol. I, p. 160.

[131] *American State Papers, Public Lands,* Vol. I, p. 160.

[132] Dunn's *Indiana* deals especially with the slavery question as it affected the history of Indiana.   See also Harris's *The History of Negro Servitude in Illinois,* pp. 7-15, for a summary of slave legislation and conditions in the Indiana Territory.

[133] Dunn's *Indiana,* pp. 299-301, 320-324.

[134] Quoted in Dillon's *A History of Indiana,* p. 415.

[135] Dunn's *Indiana,* p. 326.

[136] Acts of Congress of February 26, 1808, and March 3, 1811.— *United States Statutes at Large,* Vol. II, pp. 469, 659.   See also Farrand's *The Legislation of Congress for*

the Government of the Organized Territories of the United States, p. 26.

[137] Act of Congress of February 27, 1809.— *United States Statutes at Large,* Vol. II, p. 525.

[138] Adams's *History of the United States of America,* Vols. VI-IX; McMaster's *A History of the People of the United States,* Vols. III and IV, and other standard histories contain detailed accounts of this period.

[139] Dunn's *Indiana,* pp. 412, 417.

[140] *Niles' Register,* Vol. I, p. 388; and *American State Papers, Miscellaneous,* Vol. II, p. 277.

[141] *United States Statutes at Large,* Vol. III, p. 289.

[142] Dillon's *A History of Indiana,* pp. 557-559; and Dunn's *Indiana,* pp. 423-424.

[143] *United States Statutes at Large,* Vol. III, p. 399.

CHAPTER VII

[144] *United States Statutes at Large,* Vol. II, p. 309.

[145] John Reynolds in *The Pioneer History of Illinois* (Second Edition), p. 346, says: "I presume, in 1803, there were scarcely three thousand souls, French and Americans, in all Illinois. No census at that day was taken and it is difficult to be certain in the number; but judging from the best *data* in my power and my personal observation, I think the above is correct." In 1809 it was estimated that the population of the Illinois Territory was about 9,000.— Davidson and Stuvé's *A Complete History of Illinois from 1673 to 1873,* p. 245.

[146] Legislative memorials were sent to Congress in

1806, 1807, and 1808.— Davidson and Stuvé's *A Complete History of Illinois from 1673 to 1873*, p. 241.

[147] Davidson and Stuvé's *A Complete History of Illinois from 1673 to 1873*, p. 242.

[148] Davidson and Stuvé's *A Complete History of Illinois from 1673 to 1873*, p. 242; and Reynolds's *The Pioneer History of Illinois* (Second edition), p. 173.

[149] Davidson and Stuvé's *A Complete History of Illinois from 1673 to 1873*, p. 242.

[150] *United States Statutes at Large*, Vol. II, p. 514. This act went into effect March 1, 1809.

[151] See Clay's letter of recommendation, in Edwards's *History of Illinois from 1778 to 1833; and Life and Times of Ninian Edwards*, p. 27.

[152] See Edwards's *History of Illinois from 1778 to 1833; and Life and Times of Ninian Edwards*, for a biography of Governor Edwards.

[153] Washburne's *The Edwards Papers* in the *Chicago Historical Society's Collection*, Vol. III, p. 17, editor's note.

[154] The original certificate of authority from the Judges is among the Governor's papers in the library of the Chicago Historical Society.— *Edwards Papers — Autograph Letters*, Vol. 50, p. 9.

[155] Brown's *Early History of Illinois* in the *Fergus Historical Series*, No. 14, pp. 100-101.

[156] Moses's *Illinois, Historical and Statistical*, Vol. I, p. 241.

[157] See correspondence in Washburne's *The Edwards*

Papers in the *Chicago Historical Society's Collection*, Vol. III.

[158] This point is illustrated by the fact that Edwards seemed to consider land speculation by a Governor as perfectly legitimate, and that he speculated continually. Both St. Clair and Harrison, as has been pointed out, considered such practices as questionable.

[159] *Executive Register for the Illinois Territory* in the *Publications of the Illinois State Historical Library*, Vol. III, p. 3.

[160] *Executive Register for the Illinois Territory* in the *Publications of the Illinois State Historical Library*, Vol. III, pp. 3-4.

[161] *Executive Register for the Illinois Territory* in the *Publications of the Illinois State Historical Library*, Vol. III, pp. 4-6.

[162] *Executive Register for the Illinois Territory* in the *Publications of the Illinois State Historical Library*, Vol. III, p. 7.

[163] Edwards's *History of Illinois, from 1778 to 1833; and Life and Times of Ninian Edwards*, pp. 28-29. The address is here printed in full, as is also the reply of the Governor.

[164] Edwards's *History of Illinois, from 1778 to 1833; and Life and Times of Ninian Edwards*, p. 33.

[165] Edwards's *History of Illinois, from 1778 to 1833; and Life and Times of Ninian Edwards*, p. 35.

[166] Edwards's *History of Illinois, from 1778 to 1833; and Life and Times of Ninian Edwards*, p. 33.

[167] See letter from John Pope, United States Senator from Kentucky, to Governor Edwards, November 9, 1809. He asked Edwards how he could justify himself if the people should elect an improper person. ''Your course would appear to be fair,'' he said, ''and calculated to give satisfaction; but I give it as my decided opinion that it will be more correct and better policy to assume the responsibility.''— Washburne's *The Edwards Papers* in the *Chicago Historical Society's Collection,* Vol. III, p. 40.

[168] See letter from Albert Gallatin, Secretary of the Treasury, to Edwards, September 8, 1809, expressing his appreciation of the difficulties of the Governor's position.— Washburne's *The Edwards Papers* in the *Chicago Historical Society's Collection,* Vol. III, pp. 46-47.

[169] Petition of over one hundred citizens of Randolph County, east of the Big Muddy River.— Washburne's *The Edwards Papers* in the *Chicago Historical Society's Collection,* Vol. III, p. 72.

[170] Edwards's *History of Illinois, from 1778 to 1833; and Life and Times of Ninian Edwards,* p. 67.

[171] *American State Papers, Indian Affairs,* Vol. I, and *Niles' Register,* Vol. II, contain many letters from Governor Edwards concerning Indian affairs. See also the *Edwards Papers.— Autograph Letters,* in the library of the Chicago Historical Society.

[172] Edwards's *History of Illinois, from 1778 to 1833; and Life and Times of Ninian Edwards,* p. 289.

[173] *American State Papers, Indian Affairs,* Vol. I, passim.

[174] *American State Papers, Indian Affairs,* Vol. I, pp. 803-804.

[175] Davidson and Stuvé's *A Complete History of Illinois from 1673 to 1873*, p. 249.

[176] Stevens's *Illinois in the War of 1812-1814* in the *Publications of the Illinois State Historical Library*, Vol. IX, pp. 72-73. A list of these forts giving their location will be found on pp. 71-72.

[177] *American State Papers, Indian Affairs*, Vol. I, pp. 797-804.

[178] Edwards's *History of Illinois, from 1778 to 1833; and Life and Times of Ninian Edwards*, pp. 38-54; and Stevens's *Illinois in the War of 1812-1814* in the *Publications of the Illinois State Historical Library*, Vol. IX, pp. 74-94.

[179] See Gomo's speech in Stevens's *Illinois in the War of 1812-1814* in the *Publications of the Illinois State Historical Library*, Vol. IX, pp. 85-87.

[180] See evidence presented in *American State Papers, Indian Affairs*, Vol. I, passim; and *Niles' Register*, Vol. II, p. 295; Vol. III, pp. 105-107; Vol. VI, pp. 113-114.

[181] *American State Papers, Indian Affairs*, Vol. I, p. 797.

[182] *American State Papers, Indian Affairs*, Vol. I, pp. 807-808. See also Stevens's *Illinois in the War of 1812-1814* in the *Publications of the Illinois State Historical Library*, Vol. IX, pp. 101-112.

[183] *American State Papers, Indian Affairs*, Vol. I, p. 808.

[184] Stevens's *Illinois in the War of 1812-1814* in the *Publications of the Illinois State Historical Library*, Vol. IX, p. 115.

[185] *Annals of Congress,* 1st Session, 12th Congress, pp. 1679-1682.

[186] See *Niles' Register,* Vol. III, p. 155 (Heald's Report) ; and Kirkland's *The Chicago Massacre of 1812.*

[187] See the *Edwards Papers — Autograph Letters,* in the library of the Chicago Historical Society; and Edwards's *History of Illinois, from 1778 to 1833; and Life and Times of Ninian Edwards,* pp. 75, 337, 346.

[188] Edwards's *History of Illinois from 1778 to 1833; and Life and Times of Ninian Edwards,* p. 75.

[189] See the following letters : Governor Edwards to William Eustis, Secretary of War, August 25 and September 6, 1812, and January 2, 1813; and Governor Edwards to Governor Harrison, August 26, 1812.— Edwards's *History of Illinois from 1778 to 1833; and Life and Times of Ninian Edwards,* pp. 337-342, 345-346.

[190] See the *Edwards Papers — Autograph Letters,* especially Vols. 49 and 50, in the library of the Chicago Historical Society; and Stevens's *Illinois in the War of 1812-1814* in the *Publications of the Illinois State Historical Library,* Vol. IX, pp. 115-169.

[191] Report of the Commissioners — *American State Papers, Public Lands,* Vol. II, p. 102. Reynolds, in *The Pioneer History of Illinois* (Second edition), p. 352, states that Michael Jones, one of the Commissioners, was excitable and irritable, and that he was easily swayed by passion and prejudice.

[192] See letters quoted in Edwards's *History of Illinois, from 1778 to 1833; and Life and Times of Ninian Edwards,* pp. 296, 306.

193 *United States Statutes at Large,* Vol. II, p. 797.

194 *Executive Register for the Illinois Territory* in the *Publications of the Illinois State Historical Library,* Vol. III, p. 7.

195 Turner's *Rise of the New West,* p. 76.

196 Pope's *Laws of the Territory of Illinois,* Vol. II, p. 673.

197 Pope's *Laws of the Territory of Illinois,* Vol. I, p. 33.

198 See Shaw's *Local Government in Illinois* in the *Johns Hopkins University Studies in Historical and Political Science,* Vol. I, No. 3, pp. 9-11.

199 *United States Statutes at Large,* Vol. II, p. 515.

200 See letter from Governor Edwards to the Secretary of War, January 26, 1812.   In a letter to R. M. Johnson on March 14, 1812, Governor Edwards stated that there were not over two hundred and twenty freeholders in the whole Territory, although the total population was 12,282 — Edwards's *History of Illinois, from 1778 to 1833; and Life and Times of Ninian Edwards,* pp. 296, 306.   See also Davidson and Stuvé's *A Complete History of Illinois from 1673 to 1873,* p. 283.

201 Edwards's *History of Illinois, from 1778 to 1833; and Life and Times of Ninian Edwards,* p. 308.

202 Edwards's *History of Illinois, from 1778 to 1833; and Life and Times of Ninian Edwards,* p. 307.

203 Act of May 20, 1812. — *United States Statutes at Large,* Vol. II, p. 741.

204 *Executive Register for the Illinois Territory* in the *Publications of the Illinois State Historical Library,* Vol.

III, p. 26; and Edwards's *History of Illinois, from 1778 to 1833; and Life and Times of Ninian Edwards*, pp. 67, 306.

[205] *Executive Register for the Illinois Territory* in the *Publications of the Illinois State Historical Library*, Vol. III, p. 28.

[206] Pope's *Laws of the Territory of Illinois*, Vol. I, pp. 33, 90-115.

[207] Quoted in Edwards's *History of Illinois, from 1778 to 1833; and Life and Times of Ninian Edwards*, p. 85.

[208] Edwards's *History of Illinois, from 1778 to 1833; and Life and Times of Ninian Edwards*, pp. 85-92.

[209] Edward's *History of Illinois, from 1778 to 1833; and Life and Times of Ninian Edwards*, p. 92.

[210] *United States Statutes at Large*, Vol. III, pp. 237, 327.

[211] *Edwards Papers — Autograph Letters*, especially Vol. 48, in the library of the Chicago Historical Society; and Washburne's *The Edwards Papers* in the *Chicago Historical Society's Collection*, Vol. III, passim. See also letters from Shadrach Bond, Delegate to Congress from Illinois, to Governor Edwards, complaining of this inattention, especially on the part of the Secretary of War, John Armstrong. — *Edwards Papers — Autograph Letters*, Vol. 48.

[212] See *United States Statutes at Large*, Vol. VII, passim.

[213] *Edwards Papers — Autograph Letters*, especially Vol. 51, in the library of the Chicago Historical Society; and Washburne's *The Edwards Papers* in the *Chicago Historical Society's Collection*, Vol. III, passim.

[214] *United States Statutes at Large,* Vol. III, pp. 428, 536.

CHAPTER VIII

[215] Act of January 11, 1805. — *United States Statutes at Large,* Vol. II, p. 309.   This act was to take effect June 30, 1805.

[216] Cooley's *Michigan,* p. 149.

[217] Letter from Governor Hull to the Secretary of State, James Madison, August 3, 1805. — *Letters and Papers from the Territory of Michigan,* Bureau of Rolls and Library, Washington, D. C.; and Cooley's *Michigan,* pp. 154, 156-157.

[218] Letter from Judge A. B. Woodward to James Madison. — *Letters and Papers from the Territory of Michigan,* Bureau of Rolls and Library, Washington, D. C.

[219] *American State Papers, Public Lands,* Vol. I, p. 249.

[220] Quoted in Farmer's *Detroit* in Powell's *Historic Towns of the Western States,* p. 105.

[221] Report of Governor Hull and Judge Woodward, October 10, 1805. — *American State Papers, Public Lands,* Vol. I, pp. 247-249.

[222] Act of April 21, 1806. — *United States Statutes at Large,* Vol. II, p. 398.

[223] Cooley's *Michigan,* pp. 156-157.

[224] *American State Papers, Public Lands,* Vol. I, pp. 248, 249.

[225] Farmer's *Detroit* in Powell's *Historic Towns of the Western States,* p. 104.

226 Governor Hull seemed to consider it a hardship that he was obliged to live at a "small farmer's house" when Detroit was in ashes and no other accommodations were to be had. See letter from Hull to James Madison, *Letters and Papers from the Territory of Michigan*, Bureau of Rolls and Library, Washington, D. C.

227 See *Letters and Papers from the Territory of Michigan*, Bureau of Rolls and Library, Washington, D. C.; *Niles' Register*, Vol. III, pp. 25, 26, 37-39, 92; Parish's *The Robert Lucas Journal of the War of 1812 During the Campaign Under General Hull*; and Winsor's *Narrative and Critical History of America*, Vol. VII, pp. 384, 428-429.

228 Letter from Judge A. B. Woodward to James Monroe, March 22, 1813. — *Papers and Records of the Territories*, Vol. I, Bureau of Rolls and Library, Washington, D. C.

229 For an account of the British military occupancy as given by an eye-witness, see Sheldon's *The Early History of Michigan*, pp. 397-408.

230 Lewis Cass had studied law in the office of Return J. Meigs and had been admitted to the bar. He had been in the Ohio legislature, and had served as United States Marshall for Ohio. He took an active part in the War of 1812 and was attached to Governor Hull's army at the time of the surrender of Detroit, for which he openly and indignantly denounced Hull. He was later an officer under General Harrison, and attained the rank of Brigadier-General. For a biography of Cass see McLaughlin's *Lewis Cass*.

CHAPTER IX

231 For an excellent résumé of these conditions and of

the services of Governor Cass, see McLaughlin's *Lewis Cass*, pp. 88-98.

[232] Lockwood's *Early Times and Events in Wisconsin* in the *Collections of the State Historical Society of Wisconsin*, Vol. II, p. 115; and McLaughlin's *Lewis Cass*, p. 122.

[233] *American State Papers, Public Lands*, Vol. I, p. 263.

[234] Report made on March 18, 1806. — *American State Papers, Public Lands*, Vol. I, p. 263.

[235] Act of March 3, 1807. — *United States Statutes at Large*, Vol. II, p. 437.

[236] *United States Statutes at Large*, Vol. II, p. 502; Vol. III, p. 724; Vol. IV, p. 260.

[237] Smith's *The Life and Times of Lewis Cass*, p. 142.

[238] Richardson's *Messages and Papers of the Presidents*, Vol. I, pp. 570-571; and McLaughlin's *Lewis Cass*, pp. 97-98.

[239] McLaughlin's *Lewis Cass*, pp. 98-99.

[240] *Papers of James Duane Doty* in the *Collections of the State Historical Society of Wisconsin*, Vol. XIII, pp. 163-219. This is the official journal of the expedition. See also McLaughlin's *Lewis Cass*, pp. 116-122.

[241] Young's *Life and Public Services of General Lewis Cass*, pp. 83-84. The number for each tribe is here given, and the total number of warriors is estimated at 8,890.

[242] McLaughlin's *Lewis Cass*, p. 131; and Smith's *The Life and Times of Lewis Cass*, p. 155.

[243] McLaughlin's *Lewis Cass*, pp. 118-120; and Smith's *The Life and Times of Lewis Cass*, pp. 127-130.

244 *United States Statutes at Large*, Vol. VII, passim.

245 Smith's *The Life and Times of Lewis Cass*, pp. 102-104.

246 Quoted in Smith's *The Life and Times of Lewis Cass*, p. 105.

247 *United States Statutes at Large*, Vol. III, p. 769. Two years later by another act of Congress the number of Councilors was increased to thirteen, out of twenty-six chosen by the people.

248 Act of February 5, 1825. — *United States Statutes at Large*, Vol. IV, p. 80.

249 Act of January 29, 1827.— *United States Statutes at Large*, Vol. IV, p. 200.

250 Lanman's *History of Michigan*, p. 227.

251 *Laws of the Territory of Michigan*, Vol. I, pp. 83, 113, 206, 255; Vol. II, pp. 115, 138.

252 Campbell's *Outlines of the Political History of Michigan*, p. 405.

253 *Laws of the Territory of Michigan*, Vol. I, p. 661.

254 *Laws of the Territory of Michigan*, Vol. II, p. 279.

255 *United States Statutes at Large*, Vol. IV, p. 200.

256 See Bemis's *Local Government in Michigan and the Northwest* in the *Johns Hopkins University Studies in Historical and Political Science*, Vol. I, No. 5.

257 *United States Statutes at Large*, Vol. IV, p. 560. See also Cooley's *Michigan*, pp. 197-198.

258 See Cooley's *Michigan*, pp. 205-210.

259 Governor George B. Porter of the Territory of

Michigan died of cholera in July, 1834. In 1835 John S. Horner of Virginia was appointed, but he was so poorly adapted to the rigorous border Territory that the people virtually laughed him out of the country. — See Cooley's *Michigan*, pp. 212, 220-222.

[260] Act of June 28, 1834. — *United States Statutes at Large*, Vol. IV, p. 701. The country comprised within the present States of Wisconsin and Minnesota east of the Mississippi had been attached to the Territory in 1818, when Illinois was admitted into the Union.

[261] Cooley's *Michigan*, p. 210.

[262] Michigan was admitted into the Union January 26, 1837. — *United States Statutes at Large*, Vol. V, p. 144.

[263] See Cooley's *Michigan*, pp. 213-224.

CHAPTER X

[264] *United States Statutes at Large*, Vol. V, p. 10.

[265] See Pelzer's *Augustus Caesar Dodge*, pp. 11-37, for a sketch of the life of Henry Dodge.

[266] Brunson's *Memoir of Hon. Thomas Pendleton Burnett* in the *Collections of the State Historical Society of Wisconsin*, Vol. II, pp. 308-310. See also the proclamation of Governor Dodge. — Shambaugh's *Messages and Proclamations of the Governors of Iowa*, Vol. I, p. 50.

[267] Strong's *History of the Territory of Wisconsin*, p. 223.

[268] Shambaugh's *Messages and Proclamations of the Governors of Iowa*, Vol. I, p. 50.

[269] Letter from Thomas Pendleton Burnett to Governor

Dodge, October 17, 1836. — *Collections of the State Historical Society of Wisconsin*, Vol. II, pp. 308-309.

[270] Shambaugh's *Messages and Proclamations of the Governors of Iowa*, Vol. I, p. 53.

[271] Shambaugh's *Messages and Proclamations of the Governors of Iowa*, Vol. I, pp. 3-11.

[272] *Laws of the Territory of Wisconsin*, 1836, pp. 49-50.

[273] Shambaugh's *Messages and Proclamations of the Governors of Iowa*, Vol. I, pp. 12-24. The Territory of Wisconsin at this time included the country comprised within the present States of Iowa, Minnesota, and the eastern half of North Dakota and South Dakota.

[274] *Laws of the Territory of Wisconsin*, 1837-1838, passim.

[275] Shambaugh's *Messages and Proclamations of the Governors of Iowa*, Vol. I, pp. 29-32.

[276] Thompson's *A Political History of Wisconsin*, p. 46.

[277] See Thompson's *A Political History of Wisconsin*, pp. 44-47.

[278] See Tuttle's *An Illustrated History of the State of Wisconsin*, pp. 224-225; and *Journal of the Council of the Territory of Wisconsin*, 1841-1842, pp. 14-36.

[279] *Journal of the Council of the Territory of Wisconsin*, 1842-1843, p. 6; and Tuttle's *An Illustrated History of the State of Wisconsin*, p. 231.

[280] Smith's *The History of Wisconsin*, Vol. III, p. 294.

[281] Thompson's *A Political History of Wisconsin*, p. 37.

[282] *United States Statutes at Large*, Vol. IX, p. 233.

INDEX

INDEX

County Lieutenant, powers and
duties of, 24; appointment of
Todd as, 25
Court of Common Pleas, jurisdiction of, 52; composition of, 52
Courts, system of, in Northwest
Territory, 52-53; irregular
holding of, 75, 92; establishment of, in Michigan, 129
Crawford County, trouble between Dodge and people of,
146-147
Creoles, difficulties in dealing
with, 61
Crimes and punishment, law relative to, 51, 68-69, 113, 138
Currency, depreciation of, 27,
127-128

DANIEL, Walker, 163
Dearborn, Henry, letter from, 173
Delegate to Congress, experience
of Harrison as, 77; election of,
by people, 88, 112; election of,
in Indiana, 93; need for, 112;
election of, in Illinois, 113;
election of, in Wisconsin, 146-
147; Doty as, 151; experience
of Dodge as, 154
Democracy, growth of, in Old
Northwest, 22, 23; growth of,
in Indiana Territory, 88; elements of, in Michigan, 129-130
Demunbrunt, Thimothé, 28; petition from, 162; endorsement
by, 163
Des Moines County (Iowa), 149
Detroit, British possession of, 62;
establishment of land office at,
83; surrender of, by Hull, 107,
125; destruction of, by fire,
122; suffering at, 122; temporary town laid out at, 122;
land given to citizens of, 123;
reference to, 130, 131, 184;
Council House at, 138; whipping-post at, 138; population
of, 168
Dinsmore, Silas, letter to, 173
Dodge, Henry, biography of, 6;
appointment of, as Governor,
145; oath of office taken by,
145; character and experience
of, 145-146; apportionment by,
146; proclamation by, 146,
147; support of, by legislature,
147; first message of, 147-149;
second message of, 149; veto
message of, 150; character of
administration of, 150-151; Indian treaties made by, 151; removal of, 151; successor to,
151; re-appointment of, 154
Dodge, John, 163
Doty, James Duane, appointment
of, as Governor, 151; character
and experience of, 151-152;
troubles between legislature
and, 152-153; land speculations
of, 153; reasons for opposition
to, 153; removal of, 153
Duer, William, dishonesty of, 170
Dunn, J. P., 80

EDUCATION, provisions of Ordinance relative to, 32; provisions
for, in Wisconsin, 149
Edwards, Ninian, appointment
of, as Governor, 94; birth and
early life of, 94-95; character

and ability of, 95-96; comparison of, with St. Clair and Harrison, 95, 97; popularity of, 96; positions held by, 96; commercial enterprises of, 96; apparent uneasiness of, 96; character of administration of, 97; duties of office assumed by, 97; difficulties confronting, 97-100; plan of, for militia elections, 99-100; need of action on part of, 100; interpreters employed by, 101; information concerning Indians gained by, 101; efforts of, to secure assistance, 102; memorial to, 102; confidence of people in, 102; companies of rangers raised by, 102; preparations for defense directed by, 102-103; news of Prophet's plans brought to, 103; expedition sent out by, 103; speech of, 104; difficulties of, in Indian diplomacy, 104; effort of, to conciliate Indians, 104; report of, concerning dangers from Indians, 106; frontier forces strengthened by, 107; remonstrances of, 108; inability of, to secure aid from Kentucky, 108; differences of opinion between Harrison and, 108-109; preëmption law urged by, 110; legislative activities of, 110; hesitancy of, to call election, 111-112; desire of, for Delegate to Congress, 112; extension of suffrage advocated by, 112; curtailment of powers of,

113; election called by, 113; views of, requested by legislature, 114; harmony between other branches of government and, 114; difficulties of, in securing government aid, 114-115; Indian treaties made by, 115; duties of, as Superintendent of Saline, 115-116; influence of, 116; loyalty of, to Illinois, 116; attitude of, toward governorship, 116; later life of, 117; attitude of, toward speculation, 177

Electors, qualifications of, 34

England, desire of, to humble France, 16, 17; governmental transformations in, 17; rule of colonies by, 17

English, character of settlements of, 16; border warfare between French and, 17; victory of, over French, 17; unfriendly policy of, 19; alliances of, with Indians, 19; failure of, to relinquish western posts, 20; sinister influence of, 20; Indians encouraged by, 20; character of government of West by, 24; friendliness of Indians to, 29; unfriendliness of, to Americans, 62; Indians incited by, 62, 63, 100, 124, 127; land grants made by, 62, 83; evidence of influence of, over Indians, 105; rule of, in Michigan, 125; difficulties with, in Michigan, 134-136; American vessels searched by, 136

Europe, American counterparts of wars in, 17

Eustis, William, letter to, 180

FLORIDA, Spanish settlements in, 16; cession of, to England, 17

Force, Peter, account written by, 163

Fort Dearborn, soldiers at, 107; massacre at, 107

Fort Duquesne, capture of, 17

Fort Madison, soldiers at, 107

Fort Massac, soldiers at, 107

Fort Recovery, 75

Forts, description of early, 102-103

Fox River, improvement of, 147-148

France, territory ceded by, to England, 17; territory ceded by, to Spain, 17; elimination of, from North America, 17; effect of policy of, 18-19

Franklin (Missouri), 96

French, early explorations and settlements of, 16; chain of forts built by, 16; alliances of, with Indians, 16; border warfare between English and, 17; victory of English over, 17; encumbrances inherited from, 19; character of government of West by, 24; land grants made by, 62, 83; settlements by, 92

French and Indian War, St. Clair in, 48

French settlers, indifference of, to government, 27, 129; attitude of, toward Virginia, 29; destitute circumstances of, 60,

127; difficulties in dealing with, 61, 63; employment of, by Edwards, 101; confusion of land titles of, 124

Frontiersman, character of, 22-23

GALLATIN, Albert, letter from, 178

Gibson, John, executive functions exercised by, 89

Gomo, Levering received by, 103; speech by, 104, 106

Governor, Provincial, opposition to, 39; similarity of Territorial Governor to, 39, 46

Governor, Territorial, importance of, 8, 9; influence of, 22; appointment of, 32, 42-43; term of, 32, 42-43; qualifications of, 32-33; legislative functions of, 33, 44-45; administrative duties of, 33, 44; military duties of, 33; elections called by, 34, 44; relation of, to legislature, 34, 35; veto power of, 35, 36; change in manner of appointment of, 38; Secretary to act in absence of, 38; type of, provided by Ordinance, 39; control by, well suited to West, 41; evolution of type of, 42; supreme power of, 42; source of power of, 43; responsibility of, 43, 45-46; reports of, 43; residence and property qualifications of, 43; salary of, 43, 165; duties of, as Superintendent of Indian Affairs, 43; appointive power of, 44; counties laid

75; population of, 75; government provided for, 76; provision for legislature in, 76; development of, 76-77; Harrison first Governor of, 77; advantages of, 77; organization of government in, 77; popularity of Harrison in, 78; laws of Northwest Territory adopted by, 78; method of enacting laws in, 79; source of laws of, 79; dominance of Virginia statutes in, 79; judicial procedure modified in, 80; clash of jurisdictions in, 80; difficulties caused by revision of judicial system in, 80; administration in, 81; local government in, 81; provision of act creating, 82; conduct of Indian affairs in, 82-83; land troubles in, 83-85; country west of Mississippi attached to, 85; question of slavery in, 85-86; change in sentiment of, 86; second stage of government in, 86-87; choice of Councilors in, 87; history of last years of, 88; extension of right of suffrage in, 88; advanced character of, 88-89; part of, in War of 1812, 89; Posey appointed Governor of, 89; influence of Harrison in, 90; growth of population of, 90; claims of, for statehood, 90; constitutional convention in, 90; saneness in development of, 91; division of, 92, 119;

opposition to division of, 93; excitement over division of, 93; reference to, 94, 116, 119, 120, 145; animosities caused by division of, 97; concentration of troops in, 108; laws of, adopted in Illinois, 110, 113; privileges granted to people of, 112

Indians, French trade with, 16; futility of consigning West to, 18, dealings of English with, 19; resistance of, to western settlement, 20; encouragement of, by English and Spanish, 20; effect of presence of Clark upon, 27; friendliness of, to English, 29; inciting of, by English, 62, 100, 127; hostility of, to white settlers, 63, 100; presents given to, by English, 63; terror caused by, 64; dealings of St. Clair with, 64; defeat of St. Clair by, 65; defeat of, by Wayne, 65; dealings of Harrison with, 82-83; importance of land cession by, 82; troubles with, in Illinois Territory, 100-109; land titles of, 124; dealings of Hull with, 124; subduing of, by Cass, 128; number of, in Michigan, 132; troubles with, in Michigan, 132-134; dealings of Dodge with, 151

Internal Improvements, works of, in Michigan, 132, 140; Dodge's recommendations for, 147-148

Philadelphia, constitutional convention at, 31-32

Pilgrims, landing of, 16

Plains of Abraham, English victory on, 17, 118

Polk, James K., accession of, to presidency, 154; Dodge re-appointed by, 154

Pope, John, 178

Pope, Nathaniel, appointment of, as Secretary, 97; executive functions exercised by, 97

Porter, George B., death of, 186

Posey, Thomas, appointment of, as Governor, 89; reference to, 90

Pottawattamies, chief of, 103, 106; council of Edwards with, 106

Prairie du Rocher, trial at, 166

Preëmption, right of, granted, 110, 131; right of, urged by Dodge, 147

President of the United States, Territorial officers appointed by, 38; Councilors selected by, 70; appointive power of, curtailed, 88; memorial to, 102

Proclamation of 1763, provisions of, 17, 18; futility of, 18

Property, provisions of Ordinance relative to descent and transfer of, 32

Prophet, The, Indians aroused by, 103, 105, 106

Public lands, difficulties in disposition of, 27; difficulties of St. Clair in settling claims to, 62-63; act relative to sale of, 77-78; difficulties of Harrison in settling claims to, 83, 84; troubles relative to, in Illinois, 109-110; difficulties concerning, in Michigan, 124, 130; new policy relative to, 130; extinguishment of Indian title to, 132; recommendations of Dodge concerning, 147

QUARTER Sessions, jurisdiction of, 52; composition of, 52; duty of justices of, 53

RAISIN River, settlers from, 127

Randolph County, (Illinois), establishment of, 97; address by citizens of, 98; petition of people of, 178

Receivers of Public Moneys, appointment of, 83; duties of, 83; work of, 84-85

Registers, appointment of, 83; duties of, 83; work of, 84-85

Representatives, Territorial, elections of, 34, 70; qualifications of, 34, 111; term of, 34; members of Council nominated by, 34; legislative functions of, 34-35; people given right to elect, 112

Revolutionary War, 7; English settlements at time of, 16; measures foreshadowing, 17, 18; western phase of, 18, 19, 20; St. Clair in, 48

Robertson, James, letter to, 173

Rock River, improvement of navigation of, 148

Roosevelt, Theodore, 21

Russell, Colonel, troops of, 108

feat of, 170; letter of dismissal to, 171

St. Clair County (Illinois), establishment of, 97; militia company in, 101; mass meeting of citizens of, 102

St. Clair County (Northwest Territory), establishment of, 53

St. Lawrence River, chain of forts connecting Mississippi and, 16; reference to, 119

St. Louis, 96

Salt Works, supervision of, 115-116

Sargent, Winthrop, list of settlers prepared by, 161

Scott, Governor, failure of, to send troops, 108

Secretary, Territorial, appointment of, 33; term of, 33; qualifications of, 33; change in manner of appointment of, 38; added powers of, 38; salary of, 165

Settlement, manner of, 21-22; cheap land an incentive to, 22

Settlers, desire of, for strong government, 41; desire to protect, 41; methods of, in preserving order, 49; needs of, 60; number of, in Northwest Territory, 60; location of, 60; efforts of St. Clair to relieve, 60-61; hostility of Indians to, 63-64; politics of, 72; difficulty in settling land claims of, 83-85; means of protection for, 102-103; uncertainties of, as to land policy, 109-110; right of preëmption for, 110, 131;

character of, in Illinois, 111; condition of, in Michigan, 127, 128

Shambaugh, Benj. F., editor's introduction by, 5; acknowledgments to, 10

Shawnees, leader of, 103, 105, 106

Shelby, Isaac, failure of, to send troops, 108

Slavery, prohibition of, in Ordinance, 32, 85; attitude toward, in Indiana Territory, 85; attitude of Harrison toward, 86; change of sentiment relative to, 86

Soldiers, number of, in Illinois country, 107

South, Old Northwest settled by people from, 21

Southern States, influence of, in Northwest, 53, 54; laws from, 79; people from, in Illinois, 110, 116

Southwest, manner of settlement of, 21; settlers from, in Northwest, 49

Spain, Florida ceded to England by, 17; territory ceded to, by France, 17

Spaniards, early explorations and settlements of, 16; intrigues of, against Americans, 19, 62; Indians aided and encouraged by, 20

Speculators, designs of, frustrated, 71

Springfield (Illinois), 96

Statehood, preparation for, in West, 8; provision for, as incentive to progress, 37; movement for, opposed by St. Clair, 72; triumph of, 73; question of, in Wisconsin, 154

States, admission of, provided for by Ordinance, 32, 37-38

Suffrage, extension of right of, 88, 112-113, 138

Superintendent of Indian Affairs, 96; activities of Edwards as, 115; Hull's activities as, 124; activities of Cass as, 132-134

Superintendent of the United States Saline, 96; duties of Edwards as, 115-116

Supreme Court, Territorial, composition of, 52; jurisdiction of, 52; difficulty in convening, 66; power given to single judges of, 67; place of sittings of, 67

Symmes, John Cleves, property owned by, 56; attitude of, toward St. Clair, 56; queer proposition made by, 167; St. Clair's resignation requested by, 167

TALLMADGE, Nathaniel P., appointment of, as Governor, 153; character and training of, 153; administration of, 153-154; removal of, 154

Territorial government, distinctive character of, 8; importance of study of, 8; foundation for, 24; first stage of, 32-33; provisions for second stage of, 33-35; participation of people in, 35, 37; control of, by National government, 36; advantages of

citizens under, 36-38; factors in determining character of, 40-42; reasons for centralization in, 42; lack of precedents for, 66; second stage of, in Northwest Territory, 69-70; fortunate beginning of, 74; character of, in Indiana, 76-77; establishment of, in Indiana, 77; desire for second stage of, in Indiana, 86; establishment of second stage of, in Indiana, 87; reasons for delaying second stage of, in Illinois, 111-112; adoption of second stage of, in Illinois, 113; second stage of, voted down in Michigan, 130; second stage of, established in Michigan, 136; policy of altering, 138

Tippecanoe, effect of victory of, 105, 106, 124

Todd, John, appointment of, as County Lieutenant, 25; instructions to, 25; early life of, 26; arrival of, at Kaskaskia, 26; duties of office assumed by, 26; order issued by, 27; difficulties confronting, 27; efforts of, to carry on government, 27; departure of, from Illinois County, 28; unwarrantable criticism of, 28; apologetic letter to, 28; land grants by successors of, 62

Todd, Thomas, 97

Town-meeting, absence of, in early history of Northwest, 53-54; establishment of, 54